# 7 Nights of Slow Cooking

SLOW
COOKER
CENTRAL

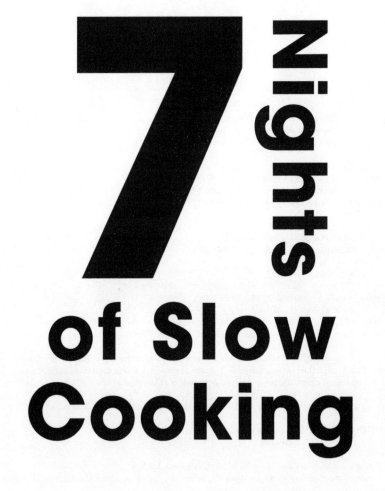

7 Nights
of Slow
Cooking

Paulene Christie

ABC
BOOKS

The ABC 'Wave' device is a trademark of the Australian Broadcasting Corporation and is used under licence by HarperCollins*Publishers* Australia.

**HarperCollins*Publishers***
Australia • Brazil • Canada • France • Germany • Holland • India
Italy • Japan • Mexico • New Zealand • Poland • Spain • Sweden
Switzerland • United Kingdom • United States of America

First published in Australia in 2022
by HarperCollins*Publishers* Australia Pty Limited
Level 13, 201 Elizabeth Street, Sydney NSW 2000
ABN 36 009 913 517
harpercollins.com.au

A catalogue record for this book is available from the National Library of Australia.

ISBN 978 0 7333 4232 5 (paperback)
ISBN 978 1 4607 1463 8 (ebook)

Cover design by Mietta Yans, HarperCollins Design Studio
Cover images: Braised Sirloin Roast With Vegetables by Jeff Wasserman/stocksy.com/1275918; all other images by istockphoto.com
Author photograph by Karlie Holloway
Typeset in Adobe Jenson Pro by Kirby Jones
Printed and bound in Australia by McPherson's Printing Group

*Simon, Caleb, Talyn & Ella*
*As long as we have each other, we have everything*
*xx*

# Contents

## Set 5        89

Fast 'n' Easy Chicken Soup, Buffalo Chicken Meatballs, Saucy Sweet Pork Steaks, Spaghetti Bolognaise, Chicken and Leek Pie, Shredded Beef Ragu, Roast Lamb Obsession

## Set 6        101

Tomato and Bacon Soup, Pasta Bake, Steak in Creamy Mushroom Sauce, Lamb Surprise, Oyster Asian Chicken, Whole Chicken Korma, Marinated Roast Beef

## Set 7        113

Pumpkin and Sweet Potato Soup, Rissoles in Rich Gravy, Sweet Lamb Curry, Whole Chicken with Garlic Butter and Soy, Asian Beef Udon Noodles, Beef Stroganoff, Rolled Turkey Roast and Vegetables

## Set 8        125

Classic Pea and Ham Soup, Pickled Pork, Tuscan Meatballs, Steak Diane, Sticky French Chicken, Thai Red Curry Pork Fillet, Roast Lamb with Rosemary Butter and Red Wine

## Set 9        137

Chicken Laksa Soup, Philly Cheesesteaks, Sweet and Sour Pork Sausages, Classic Curried Mince, Chinese Lamb Steaks, Coq au Vin, Roast Pork and Amazing Crackle

## Set 10        151

Creamy Smooth Vegetable Soup, Chinese Chicken, Rich Sausage Hotpot, Rainbow Frittata Slice, Classic Silverside, Moroccan Lamb Mince with Lemon Couscous and Minted Yoghurt, Mississippi Pot Roast

## Set 11        163

Chinese Chicken Noodle and Sweetcorn Soup, Honey Soy Pork Rashers, Cheesy Chicken and Broccoli Pasta, Chilli Con Carne, Honey Mustard Chicken, Beef Cheeks in Guinness Gravy, Classic Roast Lamb

## Set 12        175

Minestrone Soup, Silverside in Soft Drink, Lemongrass Chicken, Carolina BBQ Pork Chops, Sweet Chilli BBQ Whole Chicken, Oriental Beef Lettuce Bowls, Pork Belly in Apple Cider

# INTRODUCTION

## Hello!

It's great to see you again.

Come in, make yourself at home.

I'll give you the grand tour.

Welcome to book seven in the Slow Cooker Central series – 7 *Nights of Slow Cooking*!

As with all our books, here we have an amazing collection of slow cooker recipes for you and your family. Great, easy, tasty, nutritious, and delicious home cooking! However, we have also added a new element to this edition that we are so excited to share with you – meal plans and shopping lists!

Let me explain…

Has anyone noticed how we have to cook dinner EVERY night of the week – seven nights? Ha-ha, it's a lot some weeks right!? With this edition we are focusing only on dinner recipes. Dinner time is such a hectic time in so many households and we want to bring you the ultimate guide to overcoming that daily dinner dilemma. With 7 *Nights of Slow Cooking* we are going to take the hard work out of that daily 'what to cook for dinner' saga and make it easy.

In this book you will find recipes grouped into sets of seven – one recipe for each evening of the week. Each set includes easy step-by-step instructions for each fabulous dinner *and* its own complete shopping list!

There are so many benefits to planning your menu and shopping in advance. Planning helps us decide now what we will do later, so there's no last-minute panic around what to cook, what to cook it with, or racing to the shops for some last-minute elusive ingredient you thought you had, but didn't. We can all fall back to our trusted, repeated regulars at mealtimes just because they are easy or familiar, but another wonderful thing about menu planning is that it brings more variety to your meals and ingredients. What's more, by taking the time to plan menus ahead at the start of the week, you can then shop just once and in an organised way. It will save you time, save you money, and save you stress! Imagine – no more wandering the shops aimlessly looking for inspiration and ingredients on the fly and no more multiple mid-week shop dashes.

Let's discuss how it all works ….

## How to cook with 7 Nights of Slow Cooking

In these pages you will find 15 weeks, or sets, of nightly meals all ready for you to enjoy. Each set includes seven tasty dinners for you and your family. Imagine a soup one night, a Saturday night showstopper for when you have a little more time to tinker in the kitchen, a Sunday roast and four other delicious dinners to bring new variety, new tastes and new simplicity to your weekly dinner routine.

Each set includes a couple of your all-time trusted favourites returning, so that while trying lots of new recipes, you still get to enjoy the ones you love! We've even included a bonus desserts chapter for when you need to soothe that sweet tooth or deliver a knockout dessert after dinner!

Choose a set, or choose multiple sets and get ready to go shopping! Each shopping list has all the ingredients that you'll need for the seven recipes.

Each recipe has suggestions for what might accompany the main dish. But we know that different families enjoy different side dishes with their dinner. When you choose your set, sit down and read through each one and add to the shopping list either the suggested side ingredients or what you'll need based on your tastes to round out your shop.

Before you shop, check off the items you already have on hand and don't need to buy more of to make your shopping day even easier. Be sure to check out the list of pantry staples on page 31 which covers many of these common and versatile items.

Then just like that, dinner is sorted for the whole week!

In the next chapter we've included lots of handy tips on shopping, prepping and storing in bulk so, if you like to plan ahead, why not choose a few sets at a time to shop for.

While I slow cook almost every night of the week, I understand not everyone wants to. That's the beauty of these sets! Once you have all the ingredients for a set, you know that whether you want to cook those seven recipes over the week, over a fortnight, or even over several weeks – you can open any page in that set and know everything is right there ready for you! It doesn't get any easier ☺

# Menu Planning & Shopping Tips

*Planning helps us decide now what we will do later. This means more time for life outside the kitchen and a whole lot less stress!*

## Benefits of menu planning

- Streamline your routine by knowing when you will plan, shop and prep.
- Make the family budget easier to plan and more cost-effective.
- Your family can see ahead of time what is on the menu. Not only will that save you the endless 'what's for dinner?' conversations, but they can step in and help on days you may be busy or delayed. Just ask anyone in your family to pick up the book, turn to the page you are cooking that day and follow the easy instructions to cook dinner themselves. It's not all on you!
- Prevent dinner time boredom! Grow your cooking skills, explore new tastes, and get out of the rut of cooking the same old meals on endless repeat.
- Get the whole family involved in choosing the menu set for the week, or the order of how you cook them – then everyone gets to be a part of it!
- Enjoy less stress, less anxiety, and less decision fatigue at the dinnertime burnout hour at the end of every day. Decisions are already made and everything you need is ready to go. Feel prepared!
- Avoid wasted ingredients from planning vague meal ideas that never end up getting cooked, which means ingredients then spoil or go to waste. Have a plan and waste nothing!
- Once you have your menu plan you may also like to prep some ingredients in advance. Peel, chop, and prep some of the ingredients the night before or on weekends to make putting dinner in the slow cooker on the day even easier.
- Menu planning not only enables you to shop more easily, but it also makes it so much simpler to order your groceries online too. Your list is all ready to go! Shop from the comfort of your home and avoid carpark stress, transport expenses and impulse purchases you may have made if you'd shopped in person.

- Inspire your friends. They will see you so organised with your meals and want to know your secrets 😋
- If you are watching your diet, planning meals ahead of time helps with portion control and limits last minute convenience choices and impulse fast-food purchases. If you are someone who tracks/journals your eating, having the weekly plan allows you to do that in advance to help you stay on track and achieve your goals. Investing the time in your planning is an investment in your health!

## Shopping tips

- Plan the easiest way to shop for you – online or in person or even click and collect direct from local shops. These days we are given so many great options to choose from.
- Planning your menu in advance enables you to buy some items in bulk and this brings lots of savings. You save money on the product itself as well as saving on fuel/transit by reducing extra shopping journeys. You also help the environment by reducing packaging in bulk buys.
- Incorporate weekly sales into your shopping plan. Knowing exactly what you will need allows you to shop around and grab yourself a bargain with the weekly sales or coupon incentives.
- Buy only what you need. No more watching that unused produce that you 'meant to use this week' die a slow, neglected death in your crisper.
- Compare items with the same price-per-weight and choose the best value choice. While it's great to buy in bulk, don't go too big if you aren't likely to use the product (or safely store it) by its use-by date.
- Remember your sides. Plan in advance what vegetables, pastas, or salads etc you will be serving with each meal and include them in your shop too.
- Include the non-food items you'll need in your shop – things like baking paper, aluminium foil, freezer bags and clip seal bags, toothpicks, and so on. Our pantry staples list on page 31 is a great reminder of these.
- Remember to purchase storage containers/trays too as they are great if you are prepping and or cooking in bulk or storing your leftovers for lunches etc the following day. Choose ones that are freezer and microwave safe for ease of storing and reheating

- Consider saving even more time by purchasing items that will save you time on prep – for example, frozen vegetables already chopped and ready to use. Frozen diced onion is one of my favourite time savers!

## Storage tips

- If transferring bulk items into new storage tubs, be sure to note use-by dates on the new containers for easy reference
- Consider where to store. For example, while some fresh produce is fine in fruit bowls or in the pantry, other items need to be kept in the fridge. You can always do a quick check online for information on any item you are unsure of. Store bananas alone as they can speed up the ripening of other fruit nearby and cause it to spoil before you can use it.
- Store items like grains, flours, sugars, pastas, legumes, spices and other dry ingredients in airtight sealed containers
- When appropriate, portion larger items and freeze for later what you don't need immediately. Items like some nuts and vegetables, milk and other suitable dairy products, meats and cheeses are great to portion in this way.
- Be mindful of food safety. Store raw meat always on the bottom of the fridge to prevent any raw liquids dripping on other food and posing a food safety risk. Keep cooked meats separate from raw meats.
- If you wash your produce, do so as soon as you bring it home so it's all done before you store it. That way it's all ready to use when you need it.
- Consider the containers you store in. Square containers stack better and take up less space than round ones.
- When storing leftovers try using a container that is safe to use in the freezer, microwave and if necessary, dishwasher, so the same container can be used for storing and reheating with no extra dishes needed. Also keep a good stock of freezer bags and clip seal bags on hand.
- Consider keeping a store of long-life milk and cooking cream in the cupboard for times when you have run out of the fresh variety.
- You may like to store some vegetable offcuts and ends in your freezer to make homemade vegetable stock with later. Stock liquid can then be frozen in ice cube trays. Pop the cubes into a bag to use in your next recipe. Tomato paste concentrate is another item that is great frozen in ice cube trays then popped into a bag ready to use when needed.

- Use bag sealers or other containers to store open bags of dry items to avoid spills and wastage.
- Label leftovers with the name of the meal and the date you cooked it, so you know what you are eating later and that it's safe to do so.
- Consider investing in a food saver/vacuum sealer. The small investment now will pay off later with less food spoilage and wastage. These food packages are also a great way of using your precious freezer space more efficiently.
- Store fresh herbs as if they were fresh flowers. Stand them upright in a tall glass with just a small amount of water in the bottom for the roots and freshen the water each day for maximum shelf life.
- If space allows, consider planting your own herb or vegetable garden. There is nothing quite like going out and harvesting your own fresh ingredients from your garden. Not only does it taste fresher but then you only need pick just what you will use. It's also lovely to look out the window and see your beautiful garden!

# Tips & FAQs for Slow Cooking

Here we have what we hope is a great collection of tips, tricks and frequently asked questions that we have gathered from the collective experience in our slow cooking community.

We've covered some really important safety do's and don'ts to help you to get the very best out of your slow cooking experiments while minimising the risks that other cooks may unknowingly take. The section on the tea-towel trick helps explain what that strategy is all about – you will see this mentioned a lot in our recipes. It helps us make many of the unique and unusual dishes we create in our slow cookers.

So BEFORE you start cooking, have a read through the hints and tips that follow – and then your hardest decision after that will just be deciding which great recipe from the book to cook first.

## Can I use frozen meat in the slow cooker?

This is a hotly debated topic. The short answer is no – you should not! Many people will tell you they have done so for years and it's never hurt them. However, that's probably more to do with luck than anything else. Don't follow dangerous advice. It's a risk that is quite frankly unnecessary, and we hope is one that you won't take for yourself or those being served your meals. Here's why...

### Health concerns

Although some people will state that they cook frozen meat in their slow cookers, the health and food technology experts say that, for food safety reasons, you should bring your food to temperatures of 60°C (140°F) or more as quickly as possible. Some people assume that cooking frozen meat in a slow cooker works the same way as with other methods, but they are not the same. Food cooked in the oven or on a stovetop heats up much faster than in a slow cooker. Cooking frozen meat in a slow cooker significantly increases the time it takes for food to reach the safe temperature target, and thus significantly increases the chances of you and your family getting food poisoning.

### Cooker care

Cooking meat from frozen also increases the risk of a ceramic slow cooker bowl cracking as a result of the wide difference in temperature between the frozen food and the heating bowl. If the bowl cracks, your slow cooker is unusable.

On a similar note, you should always remove the food from your slow cooker dish before refrigerating it. The nature of the thick ceramic bowl means it retains heat and thus takes a lot longer to cool down to safe refrigeration temperatures, once again leaving your food too long in the danger zone.

### In summary

Please don't prioritise convenience over safety. It may be that you have to take the time to defrost your meat first, or you may in fact have to leave the meal you had planned to cook for today until tomorrow when you can have the meat defrosted – but it's worth it. I for one will not take that risk with my loved ones. You are free to weigh up this risk for you and your family and hopefully make the safe decision for your home. Cook smart – cook safe.

## How can I thicken slow-cooker recipes with a high liquid content?

Slow cooking can produce dishes with excess liquid because of condensation forming on the lid and the fact the lid stays closed so the liquid doesn't reduce as with some stovetop or oven methods. Here's a collection of tips and trick you can use to ensure a thickened consistency for your final dish.

### Cornflour (cornstarch)

Mix 1–2 tablespoons of cornflour with 1–2 tablespoons of cool tap water until it becomes a thin runny paste without any lumps (some people prefer to use rice flour or arrowroot flour). Pour this mix straight into your slow cooker dish 20–30 minutes before serving and stir briefly around whatever is in the pot. Then leave the dish to continue cooking, preferably on HIGH but LOW if the recipe requires.

This added cornflour will thicken the liquids in the recipe. If this amount of cornflour doesn't thicken the liquids sufficiently, you can repeat the process. But take care not to add too much cornflour to your recipe – one or two additions are usually all that's needed. Some people ladle the liquid out of the slow cooker into a saucepan on the stove and add the cornflour there. How you do it is totally up to you.

## Gravy granules/powder

Substitute gravy granules for cornflour and follow the method described above. The suitability of this option will depend on the recipe and whether the addition of gravy will suit it.

## Grated potato

Grate 1–2 raw potatoes and add them to the slow cooker 45 minutes before serving. Stir them as much as you can around the solid ingredients. This will very quickly thicken the dish and the remaining cooking time will allow the potato to cook through.

Grated potato will only suit some recipes – those with vegetable or potato already in them or which would be complemented by the addition of potato.

You can use instant potato flakes in place of grated raw potato.

## Lift the lid

Another option is to remove the lid of the slow cooker or at least place it ajar for the last 30 minutes of cooking to enable the sauce to thicken through evaporation. This is not ideal because the nature of the slow cooker is to provide a sealed environment to maintain the cooking temperature – but it is an option.

## Use less liquid to begin with

A natural consequence of slow cooking is the increased moisture content thanks to the drip condensation from the lid down into the food during cooking. Many people think meat has to be covered in liquid to slow cook it, but in fact it needs very little liquid. If you find a dish is regularly ending up with far too much liquid, reduce the liquid in the initial recipe next time you cook it.

## The tea towel trick

While the tea towel trick (see the next page) is normally used when slow cooking cakes and breads, it can be used to absorb some of the condensation from the dish when following non-baking recipes. Please read the important safety information in the section regarding the tea towel trick.

### Flour toss
Tossing your meat in flour before cooking can also thicken the dish.

### Pulling/shredding
Pulling or shredding your meat at the end of the cooking time (assuming this suits the dish) will also take up a lot of the excess liquids in the pot.

## The tea towel (dish towel) trick

Quite a few of the recipes in this book will ask you to 'Cook with a tea towel (dish towel) under the lid'. The tea towel, which lies between the top of the slow cooker bowl and the lid of the slow cooker, acts to absorb condensation and stop it from dripping down into the food cooking inside. It's often used when you wouldn't want the cake or bread being cooked ending up soggy.

Note that this method has been devised by home slow cooker enthusiasts and is not recommended officially or declared a safe practice by slow cooker manufacturers. Please read the following information carefully before deciding for yourself if it's something you wish to do.

When using the tea towel trick, regular users suggest you fold up any excess fabric from the towel up onto the lid of the slow cooker, securing it to the lid handle, so it doesn't hang down over the hot outer casing of the slow cooker – this is very important for safety! A tea towel on the lid absorbs liquid during the cooking process, so it stays somewhat damp and is unlikely to burn.

If you have concerns about the fire hazards related to this practice, you can research the safety issues involved and inform yourself about the pros and cons. It is totally up to you to appraise the risks and decide whether it is safe to use the tea towel method with your slow cooker.

It is not recommended to use the tea towel in general slow cooking, but just as an optional measure to reduce liquid in a dish. If you decide to use this technique, do so only for cakes, breads and baking or recipes where water dripping is a major issue.

Please make your own decision regarding the safety of this practice. If in any doubt, do not do this. I personally recommend you don't leave your home when you are using a tea towel in this way, so that you are able to keep an eye on your slow cooker and the towel.

## How can I remove oil and fat from a slow cooker dish?

There are several methods you can use to remove oil from your dish. First and foremost, you can reduce the amount of fat going into the dish at the beginning.

### Be choosy
Choose lean cuts of meat, trim visible fat from meat and add little to no oil to your slow cooker recipes.

### Prep it
Pre-browning or sealing meat in a frying pan is one way to remove some of the fat before cooking it in the slow cooker (read more about pre-browning and sealing meat on page 17).

### Skim and discard
Perhaps the most obvious solution is to spoon that fat right out of there! Towards the end of the cooking process, the fat will often gather at the top of your dish so you can use a ladle or spoon to gently remove and discard it.

### The ice-cube trick
Placing ice-cubes briefly on top of the dish will cause the fat to 'stick to' the ice-cubes (because the lower temperature causes the fat to solidify). You can then discard the ice-cubes and the oil right along with them.

### The bread trick
Very briefly lay a piece of bread over the top of the dish. This will soak up the fat, which can be discarded with the bread or fed to a four-legged friend. But be very careful and always remove the bread with tongs, as it will be hot!

Some people use paper towel instead of bread to soak up the fats and oils, but if something is going to break down in my food, I would rather it were bread than paper.

Cool and skim

If you have the time or you are cooking a recipe in advance, you can cool the entire dish in the fridge overnight. The fat will solidify on top and you can remove it before reheating and serving the dish.

## What does the AUTO function on my slow cooker do?

Many slow cookers have LOW, HIGH, KEEP WARM and AUTO settings. The AUTO function usually means the dish will begin cooking at HIGH for approximately 2 hours, then the slow cooker will switch itself down to the LOW temperature setting. (The dial itself doesn't move and will remain pointing to AUTO.)

This feature varies with different slow cooker models and brands, so always consult your user manual.

## Are timers safe to use for slow cooking?

There is an important distinction between timers built in to a slow cooker and the wall kind that you plug into the power socket and then plug your slow cooker into.

A slow cooker with a timer function will generally switch your unit to a 'keep warm' mode after your pre-selected cooking time is complete. Most units will then only stay in this keep-warm mode for a limited number of hours for food safety reasons.

Power point wall timers, by comparison, are not recommended for slow cooking. For good reasons:

+ Some people use them to delay the start time of cooking. This means the ingredients are sitting out, not cooking, for several hours before the slow cooker turns on. It's a recipe for a food-poisoning disaster.
+ Some people use them to turn off the slow cooker completely at the end of the cooking time. This means your finished hot – and slowly getting cooler – dish is sitting out multiplying nasty bacteria in it until you get around to eating it. Again a recipe for a food-poisoning disaster. You would not cook a meal in your oven then just leave it in there or sitting on the kitchen bench for hours before eating it. A slow cooked meal is no different.

Definitely avoid timers designed for light fittings. These timers are not made to handle the load of a slow cooker. They could cause the slow cooker to burn out the element, or the timer itself could burn out or catch fire.

Cook smart, cook safe – please do not use wall timers for slow cooking.

## Is it safe to leave my slow cooker unattended all day while I am out of the house?

In short, usually yes ... with precautions.

Slow cookers are designed to run all day unattended without posing a fire hazard. There are, however, further precautions you can take if you're concerned.

- I always place my slow cookers on top of my ceramic cooktop. This surface is designed to withstand high temperatures, after all. Just be sure never to accidentally have a hotplate turned on (I lost my first ever slow cooker to this happening when I melted its legs off!). If you don't have this option, placing the cooker on a glass-top trivet or heavy cutting board works in a similar way.
- Ensure flammable objects are not left touching or anywhere near the slow cooker.
- Move the slow cooker away from the wall and any curtains, etc.
- Do not use the tea towel method if you are out of the house.
- Always have a working smoke alarm and electrical safety switch in your home so that if you are home and the worst somehow happens, you and your family will be alerted to the danger and the electricity supply will shut off.

## Is it okay to open the lid of my slow cooker to stir my dish or check on it?

Many of us have heard the tale that each time you open the lid of your slow cooker, it adds 30 minutes to the cooking time.

In practice, I have never personally found this to be true. If I am at home I am a habitual lid-lifter, often pausing to look at, stir, taste or even smell my dish throughout the day. And if anything, my dishes often cook much faster than I might expect.

However, slow cookers rely on the slow build-up of heat to cook food to perfection. Lifting the lid during cooking lets built-up heat escape and will lower the temperature in the slow cooker. Stirring the contents allows even more heat to escape from the lower layers of the food. Once the lid is replaced, it will take some time for the food to return to its previous temperature.

So the choice is up to you. Resist if you can, or don't. You will soon come to know your own slow cooker (or if you are like me and have several, you will get to know each of their little quirks and cooking times and temps).

## Do I need to pre-brown, pre-cook or seal my meat before placing it in the slow cooker?

This is a debate that has no right or wrong answer. Some people are fierce advocates of browning meat prior to slow cooking it ... while just as many are fiercely against doing so.

At the end of the day it comes down to your own personal choice.

But let's look at the reasons on both sides of the debate so you can decide what YOU want to do.

### Reasons to brown

- Faster cooking time – meat that is pre-browned won't need as much cooking time.
- Lock in moisture – sealing the surface of the meat can seal in extra moisture.
- Increased flavour – those caramelised, brown yummy bits on the surface of your meat that come with browning have lots of flavour that would otherwise be missing from your finished dish. Browning with herbs or spices can also increase the richness of these flavours in your recipe.
- Appearance – sometimes despite no change in taste, browned meat benefits the presentation of the final dish. By contrast, meat juices released from unsealed meat can sometimes mix with sauces etc making it appear as if cream-based sauces have split, when they have not.
- Fat removal – browning meat before cooking and then discarding the liquids produced is a great way to eliminate some of the fat from your finished dish. This is especially true when browning mince or ground beef.

- Thickening – meat dredged in flour, then browned before slow cooking, will add to the thickness of the sauce in the final dish.

## Reasons not to brown

- Convenience – this would have to be the number one reason. Many of us are drawn to slow cooking by the sheer convenience of pouring a collection of ingredients into the bowl, turning on the machine and walking away. This convenience is lessened when you have to add extra steps to pre-brown.
- Time factor – pre-browning meat tends to reduce the cooking time for the recipe. This works against many slow cookers who rely on the extended slow cooking period to make it work for them, for example when they work all day.
- Less mess – while many new slow cookers allow the option to sear in the same bowl you use for slow cooking, this is not possible with the traditional ceramic bowl slow cookers. Thus browning a dish means dirtying a frying pan. Let's face it, who likes extra dishes? Not me!
- No option – we see many of our members using slow cookers when they don't have access to stoves/ovens. In this instance they do not have the option to brown their meats but shouldn't think that means they can't slow cook a dish that asks for it.

## In summary

It really is up to you.

Personally I very rarely brown – maybe 5 per cent of the time that I slow cook, and then it's almost only those recipes which call for thin strips of meat to be flour coated and browned prior to slow cooking.

Some days and with some recipes you will want to – others you'll want to just dump in your ingredients, set and forget. Neither way is right or wrong, but hopefully in these pages we have given you the information to decide what's right for you.

# Can I slow cook a whole chicken?

You sure can! And many people will tell you that having tried slow cooking chickens whole they will never cook them any other way.

Here are some tips to keep in mind.

- You don't need to add any liquids to the slow cooker with your chicken. You will be really surprised by just how much liquid a whole chicken will release during cooking! And because a slow cooker is sealed, that liquid won't evaporate.
- Cook your chicken with the breast-side down. This keeps the breast meat sitting in the liquid that's produced during cooking so it won't dry out.
- If you are concerned there is too much liquid, or if you have a spice rub etc on your chicken that you don't want to get too immersed in liquid, you may choose to elevate the chicken above the bottom of your slow cooker by sitting it on some scrunched-up aluminium foil balls, egg rings or even an inverted dish.
- When it comes to seasoning your chicken, your imagination is your only limit. Whatever spice, marinade or herbs you may use when you cook a chicken in the oven you can use just as well in your slow cooker.
- When your chicken is cooked it will be fall-apart tender! I like to get mine out in one piece by sliding two spatulas or large mixing spoons underneath both ends of the chicken and then quickly lifting it up and out onto a dish. An alternative method is to create a foil or baking-paper sling under your chicken prior to cooking. This can be used to grasp and lift the chicken out at the end of cooking. This can be a large sling design or two strips crossed over to form a basket of sorts. You can also purchase a silicone sling (often called a turkey sling). Cook the chicken with the sling in place and then simply lift it out at the end by its handles. Whatever works for you!

## Help! I accidently cooked the absorbent pad from under my raw meat...

That awful moment when you first spot it... you have made a lovely slow cooker meal and you are just giving it a little stir before you serve it, when it appears: the absorbent pad from under your raw meat has accidentally ended up in your slow cooker – and *gasp* – you've cooked it!

Oh no!

What now?

Is your meal ruined?

Do you have to throw it out?

This actually happens a lot. More than you'd realise. At least a few times a week we see a member of our Facebook group looking for advice on what to do when they realise they've done this. So our goal was to get to the bottom of it and what it means for you and your pot full of otherwise yummy slow cooked food.

## What are they?

Absorbent meat pads or absorbent meat soakers are the little packages that often sit between your raw meat and your butcher's tray. The purpose of the pad is to catch and absorb the liquid that naturally drains from raw meat and would otherwise pool in your meat tray potentially spilling out on you when it was tilted. It also helps prevent meat from sitting in a pool of raw meat juice that could breed bacteria and reduce shelf life.

The fact they are often black to begin with or soaked red with juices means that it's easier than you may think to tip your raw meat into your slow cooker from the tray without realising you have tipped in the pad as well.

## What are they made of?

The butchers who I spoke to explained that the pads are usually made from paper pulp, plant fibres or non-toxic silicone with a plastic outer layer. They explained that they are approved for use in contact with food that is intended for human consumption, which means they have to be food-safe and non-toxic. They are not digestible, which means that even if you ate one it would go right through your digestive tract.

But what about when they are cooked? Does that change things?

## Do I need to throw my meal in the bin?

The general consensus seems to be – if the pad is broken or pierced in any way, sadly yes, you should throw your meal out.

However, if the pad is intact you may decide to still eat your meal if you are comfortable doing so. A manufacturer of these pads (www.thermasorb. com.au) advises that if they are not broken then your meal is okay to eat. The poisons information hotline people agree. They report getting a lot of calls regarding this issue and advise that if the packet is broken your meal should be discarded just to be safe. However, in their experience, if the packet is intact most people will have no ill effects. From their experience, at worst those with a sensitive stomach may experience mild nausea or an unpleasant taste, but this is rare and most of their callers experience no ill effects.

So the choice is ultimately yours.

## Help! My cream has split

In our slow cooking community we often see members posting their concern over split cream in their slow cooked dishes.

### What is splitting?

A lot of people will refer to dairy products that have split as being 'curdled'. If your dairy product curdles during storage that's a problem and you should throw it out; don't use it. However, if it separates during cooking, it's more likely that it's split and that is really only a change of appearance and texture. It's still perfectly fine to eat.

### Why does it occur?

Sauces made with dairy products can split for several reasons.

+ Low fat content – dairy products with high fat content are less likely to split.
+ High heat – exposing dairy products to high heat, e.g. close to boiling, increases the likelihood of splitting.
+ High acidity – adding dairy products to recipes with elevated acidic content can also cause splitting.

### How can I prevent it?

+ Choose higher-fat versions of your dairy product rather than the low fat varieties.
+ If possible add the dairy product at the end of your cooking time rather than the beginning. You can even take it off the heat before you add it.
+ When adding cream early, try whisking a teaspoon or so of cornflour into the cream first before adding it to your dish.
+ Choose 'cooking cream' or 'creme fraiche' or double cream – these are less likely to split.
+ Allow dairy products to come to room temperature before adding them. This can also help.

- Adding cream to a water-based recipe can cause splitting. Stirring regularly helps to avoid this.

## What do I do once it's happened?

- Remember … it's okay to eat. While a dish with split cream may not look perfect, it's certainly NOT a reason to throw it out!
- If the nature of the dish allows it, try giving the food a really good stir or whisk.
- Alternatively, try stirring through a little cornflour and water slurry.

Don't be discouraged! Next time just try the preventative measures. If all else fails, eat your meal with your eyes shut and you'll never know the difference *wink*.

## Can I prepare a meal in advance and store it in the slow cooker bowl in my fridge overnight, then put it on the next morning?

Yes, you can if you wish. But it comes with risks!

Heating a cold bowl can lead to it cracking.

Also, the bowl and its contents will retain that cold for a long time and thus take even longer to reach safe temperatures once you begin cooking, placing you at increased risk of food poisoning.

A great way around this is to prepare the dish in advance but store it in the fridge in another large bowl, for example a mixing bowl. The food can then be poured into the slow cooker bowl in the morning. You still have all the convenience but without any of the risk.

## Can I add pasta to my dish?

I often get asked about adding pasta to slow cooker recipes. Can you add raw pasta to your dish, or cooked pasta? Yes you can!

The fast option is to add cooked or almost cooked pasta shortly before your meal has finished cooking. Like any pasta, you don't want to overcook it, so if it's been pre-cooked then only leave it in there long enough to heat through with the rest of the recipe. Alternatively, cook the pasta separately and serve with your slow cooker dish at plating time.

But what if you want to add raw pasta to your recipe? That's an option too. But there are some factors that you'll need to keep in mind...

+ When you add raw pasta to your recipe you need to have enough liquid to accommodate it. While cooking, the raw pasta will absorb a lot of liquid from your recipe. This is a great way to thicken your dish if that's what you want, but it can spell disaster if your dish is already fairly dry. So if you know you will be adding pasta, be sure you add enough extra liquid at the start (or with the pasta) to accommodate it – without watering down your flavours.
+ As a general rule, add raw pasta about 45 minutes prior to serving.
+ Different types of pasta may of course cook in different time frames based on size and thickness, so for the first time check it occasionally to know when it's done to your pasta preferences.

## What is the best way to clean my slow cooker bowl?

It happens to all of us sometimes! We finish cooking our recipe only to find a baked-on ring of cooked or burnt residue inside or on the base of our slow cooker. Or maybe the inner casing of your slow cooker has stains in it? Don't despair – we've got the solution!

### Basics
+ The sooner you get it off the better!
+ Avoid harsh abrasive chemicals or cleaning scourers.
+ Always unplug the unit from the power source before cleaning.

### Cleaning inside the cooking bowl
Most slow cooker bowls can simply be washed by hand in the sink. Some are okay for washing in the dishwasher. Be sure to check your manual for what is suitable for your model as not all models are dishwasher safe.

However, if you find yourself with a baked-on ring around the bowl that's hard to remove, the easiest way to get rid of it is remove the food, add water to a level above the baked-on ring and leave the slow cooker turned to LOW for a couple of hours. The ring should clean away much more easily then.

Some suggest placing a dishwasher tablet or even a denture cleaning tablet in the slow cooker while the water is heating in it for up to two hours but it is advisable to check with your user manual whether this is safe for your model.

Ceramic bowls and lids will not withstand sudden temperature changes. Do not fill the bowl with cold water when it is hot as it will crack.

Some ceramic bowls have a porous base and should not be left standing in water for extended periods because they might absorb water. It's fine to fill inside the bowl with water and leave it for any amount of time, but avoid leaving the entire bowl standing IN water.

## Cleaning inside the main casing of the slow cooker

The metal housing of the slow cooker and electrical lead should NOT be placed in water! Be sure to completely unplug your unit from the power source and allow it to cool before any cleaning.

Over time you will find some of your food will splash down into the main casing of your slow cooker – under the cooking bowl.

It is important to ALWAYS CHECK YOUR INSTRUCTION MANUAL FIRST as to how your manufacturer recommends you clean your slow cooker.

Normally, electrical cables inside the base unit are fully sealed, but you should still exercise extreme caution in cleaning this main base unit – and again, never place the unit itself in water. If you can see heating elements inside the base, do not clean or add water in this area; instead, contact the manufacturer for advice.

For those who wish to proceed with cleaning inside the main casing, here are some suggestions I have gathered from members of the Slow Cooker Central community.

- Simply wipe the spill off with a soft, damp cloth and a small amount of dish detergent, especially if the spill is fresh or new.
- Clean using a mix of baking soda and vinegar on a cloth or sponge.
- Use a chalk-based cleaning paste like Gumption, which you can find in your supermarket cleaning aisle.
- Use baking soda and lemon juice. Combine and allow to foam then apply with a soft pad, sponge or scourer.
- While a soft green scrubbing type pad scourer should be okay, please think carefully before using a stronger steel wool type scourer as you

could scratch your inner casing or bowl. A gentle sponge or rubber based scrubbing tool is ideal.

+ Some report using a thin coat of oven cleaner (a fume-free version if you can), left for an hour or so then wiped off. If doing this I would recommend wiping over a few times with a damp cloth to minimise any smells next time you use the unit. Note: oven cleaners can be caustic and may even dissolve paint on the outside of your cooker, so use sparingly and cautiously.

### Prevention is best

Rather than deal with the clean-up, try to prevent spills where you can!

+ Spray your slow cooker bowl with some non-stick cooking spray before beginning.
+ Line your slow cooker with baking paper for baked items or ones you think may stick.
+ Use a slow-cooker liner bag or even an oven bag to slow-cook your dish.
+ Follow the cooking time recommended in the recipe and avoid overcooking and burning.
+ Do not overfill your slow cooker, which would increase the likelihood of spilling and staining in the casing area.

## Should I pack my slow cooker away in summer?

As someone who slow cooks all year round, I've never been one to subscribe to the old school of thought that it's only a winter appliance. As a result, I'm often asked about what I slow cook in hot summer months. Here I'll give you some ideas…

I personally don't find one slow cooker on the go in my kitchen makes any difference whatsoever to the temperature in my house during a hot Queensland summer. But if you feel otherwise, try running your slow cooker in your garage, laundry or patio etc. It's certainly better than standing over a stove or oven in a hot kitchen, that's for sure!

Another option is to slow cook overnight or very early morning before the temperature starts to soar. Or slow cook a few meals at once so you don't have to cook again at all the next day :)

The most important determinate of summer slow cooking is the sides. Sure, you aren't likely to cook soups, hot curries or big hearty hot casseroles, but that leaves plenty of other options, and if you change what you serve on the side, you change the season of the dish! Ditch the hot vegetables, the rice and the mash or heavy pastas and serve your slow cooked meal with salads or on light wraps, as pizza toppings or even as nibble platters and with BBQ sides!

I find most of our egg based recipes to be light and summery. Who doesn't love a quiche, omelette or frittata with a lovely side salad on a hot day! Or go for one of our chicken recipes, which cover wings, chicken drumsticks or even slow cooked whole chickens which, again, go great with a salad or with wraps or BBQ-style sides. Or perhaps a seafood recipe with chips and salad – that sounds summery!

Another great option is cold cuts of roast meat! Roast pork, beef or lamb … all great served cold on a steamy hot day with a nice fresh salad. And don't forget ribs! Always delish with a light side on a hot day!

And who can go past a simple pulled meat! So easy to serve on a bread roll with salad or slaw for an easy, light summer feed,

Of course you may just prefer to skip cooking the main meals and slow cook other things like desserts, cakes or fudge.

Whatever you decide, we have it for you here in these pages to get you through those hot steamy days of summer slow cooking.

## Are there any 'diet' recipes for slow cookers?

Almost every recipe can be adapted for weight loss or to make it healthier (with some obvious dessert-type exceptions).

Ways to adapt recipes to make them more waist-friendly include:

- Choose lean. Choose leaner cuts of meat than the recipe specifies. For example, go with low-fat mince, low-fat sausages or skinless chicken.
- Brown and bin. Brown meats before you slow cook them. This gives you an opportunity to drain and discard the fat rather than include it in your slow cooking recipe. Some people even like to boil their mince before cooking to remove fat.
- Trim the fat. Remove the fat before cooking, or remove fat or skin from the completed dish before serving.

- Bulk up. Add extra vegetables to your meal. If the dish you are cooking has few or no vegetables why not add some during cooking? Or when it comes to plating up your meal, load your plate with steamed or stir-fried veg to fill you up.
- Slash the salt. Choose low-sodium options for your ingredients. Even if the recipe doesn't specify it, I often change ingredients such as soy sauce or stocks to low-sodium options to cut the salt from the overall recipe.
- Choose low fat. In the same way that you can substitute low-salt ingredients, do the same with low-fat ones. Opt for low-fat yoghurts, milks and cheese, for example – pretty much anything that has a low-fat option.
- Selecting sides. What can make or break a meal when it comes to your waistline is sides. Choose wisely and your scales will thank you. Opt for healthier options like vegetables, salads and brown rice and the impact of the main meal is less.
- Portion power. Healthy eating is largely about moderation. You can enjoy that meal you really want, without having to totally overdo it. It's better to consume small portions of the foods that you crave rather than trying to resist them totally and ending up blowing out on a binge. Match the portion sizes of the various food groups on your plate with recommendations for a balanced and healthy diet.
- Love your leftovers. Why not cook extra when you do your next slow cooker meal? Then you can portion and store leftovers into healthy-sized meals all ready to take to work or to grab when the next attack of munchies strikes. It makes you less likely to make poor choices on impulse or opt for unhealthy take-away food.
- More of the same. As with all healthy eating plans, don't forget the basics. Drink plenty of water, eat mindfully, pack heaps of variety into your meal plans, choose fresh food when you can and move more!

## Is it toxic to slow cook raw red kidney beans?

Yes, it is! But only raw beans. This does not include the canned varieties that are already cooked. A good explanation can be found at www.choosingvoluntarysimplicity.com:

'Raw kidney beans contain especially large amounts of a toxin called phytohaemagglutinin, and amazingly, eating just four or five raw or improperly cooked kidney beans can make a person extremely ill. Ingesting larger amounts can actually cause death. Other beans, including white kidney beans, broad beans and lima beans, contain the same toxin in smaller but still dangerous amounts.'

If you'd like to read further on this issue, these websites would be good starting points:

- www.choosingvoluntarysimplicity.com/crockpots-slow-cooking-dried. beans-phytohaemagglutinin/
- www.medic8.com/healthguide/food-poisoning/red-kidney-bean. toxins.html

## Slow cooking cakes

Cooking cakes in slow cookers is out of the norm for a lot of traditionalist slow cooker users, so we wanted to include some advice on what can and can't be used in cake making in your slow cooker, and also to provide some general tips for getting the most out of your slow cooker cake making.

First and foremost, as detailed on page 13, the 'tea towel trick' is very important to prevent condensation dripping on your cakes when cooking them in the slow cooker.

Slow cookers can be used to cook packet (box) cake mixes as well as your own favourite from-scratch recipe.

But what do you cook the actual cake in?

There are three options.

### 1. Line your slow cooker inner bowl and cook your cake directly in it.

When doing this I find lining the bowl with non-stick baking paper not only prevents sticking but also gives you something to hold onto so you can lift the cake out at the end of the cooking time.

### 2. Cook your cake in a metal cake tin.

If you are concerned about using a metal cake tin dry in your slow cooker (ceramic bowls in particular are unsuitable for dry cooking) simply fill the bottom of the slow cooker bowl with 2–3 cm (1 in) of water first, then sit your cake tin gently in this water.

You can also elevate the cake tin off the bottom of the slow cooker to allow heat to circulate evenly around your cake. This can be achieved by resting the cake tin on a metal trivet, on metal egg rings or even on scrunched up balls of aluminium foil.

### 3. Cook your cake in a silicone cake tin.

Silicone cake tins (full size and cupcake size) are also safe to use in your slow cooker and will not melt. After all, they are intended for the high heat of conventional ovens.

When using non-ceramic slow cooker bowls I sit my silicone cake tins/cups directly onto the bottom of the slow cooker, without water, with no concerns. But if you prefer, you can elevate your tin using the methods described above. When using a ceramic cooker bowl I again add water first.

As with all non-traditional slow cooking, be sure to check your manual first and only do what you are comfortable doing.

## Slow cooker fudge FAQs

Our members LOVE cooking fudge! We have hundreds of different varieties on the website, so you can browse for fudge online or use one of the recipes in our books. I've compiled some commonly asked questions about fudge to help you along the way.

### What type of chocolate can I use?

Any type. Change the flavour of the chocolate to change the taste of the fudge. Milk chocolate, white chocolate, hazelnut chocolate, cookies and cream chocolate ... the options are unlimited. Some members use cooking chocolate, but others say the taste is not the same, so use your judgement. (Cooking chocolate does tend to melt at higher temperatures, so regular chocolate is ideal for the lower temp of the slow cooker.) If you are using chocolate that has a liquid-type filling, e.g. Caramello, you will need to increase the chocolate amount to account for this.

### Can I add chocolate and lollies to my fudge?

Yes. You can mix or top your fudge with anything you like. Make the base fudge, stir through whatever you like to add, then pour it into the lined tin to set. For example, you could add chopped nuts, biscuits, Mars bars, lollies (candies) ... whatever you like. Or pour your fudge into your tray to set then decorate the surface with these types of toppings. Again, the options are endless.

## How do I actually cook it? Do I need to stir it?

Break up the chocolate and place it in your slow cooker. Pour over condensed milk and add the butter and vanilla. LEAVE THE LID OFF your slow cooker and turn it on low and walk away. Every 10–15 minutes just pass by and give it a stir. It's that easy. As you near the end of the cooking time you may need to keep a closer eye on it but really it's just the odd stir along the way and there is nothing else to do.

## Can I use any spoon to stir?

It's ideal to use a metal or silicone spoon when stirring your fudge. A wooden spoon can absorb some of the liquid from your fudge so it's best to avoid these. (Not to mention the fact that a metal spoon is a little nicer to lick clean!)

## My fudge has seized – how can I fix it?

If things don't go to plan, your fudge might seize, which means it turns hard and weird instead of glossy. This problem can result from water getting into the fudge – remember, lids off for fudge to avoid condensation drips. Using a wooden spoon can do the same – remember, use a metal, plastic or silicone spoon for stirring fudge. There are a few approaches our members use to rescue seized fudge. Try stirring the living daylights out of it to bring it back to glossy. Others add a little splash of milk or condensed milk or even a bit more chocolate then stir like the clappers to bring it all back together. All is not lost. This is fixable – stir stir stir!

## How do I know when it's done?

Everyone's slow cooker takes a different amount of time to cook. Simply melting the chocolate is not enough. After some time, you'll notice a very slight 'crust' on the surface as you stir, and the mixture will come away from the edges of the bowl slightly. This is the best sign that it's done. Some larger (hotter) machines may achieve this in half an hour. My 1.5 litre cooker that I use for fudge takes more like 90 minutes to achieve this. You will get to know yours.

## What do I do with it once it's cooked?

Stir through any extras you want to add, then pour your fudge into a slice tray (I use one approximately 20cm x 20cm) lined with baking paper. You can use silicone moulds instead if you choose. Smooth the surface down to flat and add any decorations you like. If nothing is being added then simply place your tray in the fridge until set – approximately four hours should do it. Then use the baking paper to lift out your fudge from the tray. Remove the paper and cut the fudge quickly. Dipping your knife into hot water first can help cut cleanly.

## How should I store my fudge?

Store your fudge in a sealed container in the fridge (make it a non-transparent container if you want to keep it from being rapidly gobbled up by the fudge fanatics in your home *wink*). The fudge will keep up to four weeks in a fridge. It can also be frozen for up to three months.

## My fudge didn't set. What did I do wrong?

Please review the above tips. One of them will most likely reveal the reason your fudge did not set. You could also try returning your fudge to the slow cooker to reheat, adding more chocolate, then cooking it for longer. Not using enough chocolate is the number one cause of fudge not setting.

# Pantry staples

One of the best ways to ease into trying new recipes is to have a supply of staple items in your pantry – on hand and at the ready for your next kitchen session.

Useful staples include:

+ Aluminium foil
+ Baking paper
+ Baking powder
+ Balsamic vinegar
+ Canned or dried fruits
+ Canned or dried vegetables
+ Canned soups: condensed cream soups in various flavours (especially cream of mushroom and cream of chicken)
+ Cheese: tasty/cheddar style (this stores great in freezer)

- Chickpeas
- Coconut cream and milk
- Cooking oil (liquid and non-stick spray)
- Cornflour (always have this on hand for thickening of recipes)
- Couscous
- Curry powder
- Dry packet soups such as French onion and chicken noodle
- Flour: plain (all-purpose) and self-raising
- Freezer bags
- Garlic: fresh or minced in jar. I like to keep both on hand as some recipes needs fresh and it has a great shelf life.
- Ginger: fresh or minced in jar
- Gravy powder/granules
- Herbs and spices: fresh in your garden, frozen in tubes or dried in jars and packets – as many as you can gather! I like to grow my own basil, rosemary, parsley, mint, chives and green onions and then I also have an extensive collection of dried herbs.
- Honey and syrups
- Lentils
- Mustard powder
- Parmesan: fresh or dried
- Passata (a tomato-based liquid you'll find near the pasta sauces)
- Pasta
- Pepper
- Powdered milk or UHT milk
- Rice
- Salt
- Sauces: sweet chilli, BBQ, tomato, Worcestershire, soy, mint, oyster, hoisin
- Stock: powder, cubes or long life liquid (especially beef, chicken and vegetable)
- Sugar: brown and white
- Sweetened condensed milk
- Tinned tomatoes
- Tomato paste concentrate (single use sachets or larger jars/tins)
- Toothpicks
- Vinegar: white, brown and rice wine vinegar

- Wine: basic red and white for cooking (alcohol-free is fine if you prefer)
- Yeast

This is by no means an exhaustive list but it's a great start!

## Slow-cooking party food

We all know how hectic hosting parties can be!

The host is always running around trying to see to everyone's needs, having spent days trying to come up with party food ideas and then finding the time to prepare them.

There is help at hand … your slow cooker is your party helper! There are two ways your slow cooker can help:

- Use it to cook your party food before the event. Heaps of great party food recipes are also slow cooker recipes.
- Use your slow cooker to self-serve directly from on party day. Pulled meats, meatballs, chicken wings, chillis, curries and so many more options are great self-serve options with simple sides, bread rolls or even toothpicks.

Some important safety reminders:

- Place hot cookers to the back of food tables so little fingers can't accidently touch them.
- Ensure power leads are out of the way and guests can't trip on them.
- As guests arrive, especially those with little ones, show them the slow cooker table and let them know that the cookers are hot so they can be sure to keep their little ones' fingers away.
- Keep an eye on the cookers and turn them off as soon as they are empty of food.

Other slow cooker party tips:

- Borrow extra cookers from your friends if you need to.
- Label each cooker with a little card in front so guests know what's in each one.

- Provide serving plates/cups and cutlery and napkins so everything is on hand to serve.
- Make sure all the dishes are ready to eat from when the first guests arrive to ensure that no one eats anything not fully cooked.
- Alternatively, keep some slow-cooked dishes in reserve to bring them to the table only when ready to eat.
- Tell all of your guests about the great books where they can find all your recipes *wink* ha-ha!
- Sit back and enjoy your party knowing that the food is all taken care of!

# Slow-cooking on a budget

### Money $ Money $ Money

It makes the world go round they say. We all want more of it, or at least, we want to make better use of the money we already have. We are always looking to save more and slow cooking saves you money in so many ways! Let's look at how...

### Save money on cooking costs!

Slow cooking is certainly cheaper than running other appliances like ovens.

Of course, there are many variables to consider including the size and model of your slow cooker and size and efficiency of your conventional oven, but overall the stats are well in favour of your slow cooker being the cheaper way to cook – even if it takes more than eight hours instead of one hour!

Energy provider Ergon Energy advises that a slow cooker costs 4 cents per hour to run, while an oven costs 60 cents per hour.

So running your slow cooker for eight hours will cost 32 cents compared with 60 cents for just one hour of the oven (and that doesn't even account for oven pre-heating time).

More money in your pocket right there!

### Save money on shopping costs at your butcher

Slow cooking saves you money at the butcher. The very nature of long slow cooking means your end result will still be lovely and tender. So you can buy a much cheaper cut of meat rather than top shelf cuts. That's more money in your pocket!

### Cook in bulk and save!
A lot of slow cooker fans are cooking bigger meals and storing leftovers.

Many people, if they are using a large slow cooker like a six litre bowl to cook a soup, will fill it and store leftovers for another day.

The trend of freezer meal/dump bags for slow cooking is another easy way to buy ingredients in bulk to save money!

### Save money on take-away and impulse buys!
Who hasn't got to the end of a long day and out of sheer exhaustion just decided to grab take-away for dinner instead. We've all been there! Throw in some tired, hungry kids into the mix and it's a recipe for disaster.

So save yourself and slow cook! Come dinner time, you'll have dinner all ready cooked, smelling amazing and just ready to serve. It's actually faster and easier than going out for take-away …. and so much cheaper on the hip pocket!

### Save money with smart choices!
Some recipes are going to be more budget-friendly than others based on their core ingredients. Choose wisely and you can immediately start saving money. For example, skip the seafood and prime steak options and instead head to recipes using sausages, mince, vegetables, chicken and soups.

### Use leftovers in a new meal!
For example, use a moist meat or meat and veg meal from the night before to make a pie for the next night.

So why wait? Get slow cooking and save money right away!

## Goodbye, oven. Hello, slow cooker! Converting oven and stovetop recipes for your slow cooker

Now you're hooked on slow cooking, I bet you'll find there are heaps of your family's favourite recipes that you have always cooked in the oven or on the stovetop that you want to convert for a slow cooker. And, for almost all of them, there is no reason you can't!

Here are some simple pointers:

+ Reduce the amount of liquid. The condensation that forms in your slow cooker when in use means that recipes cooked in slow cookers need much less liquid then their traditional stovetop or oven counterparts. As a general rule try reducing the total liquid by approximately one third.
+ Use cheaper cuts of meat. Remember that almost any cut of meat – even the cheapest and toughest – is sure to be tender after slow cooking. So feel free to replace more expensive cuts of meat with a cheaper option.
+ Adjust the time. See the chart below to convert your stove and oven times to slow cooker times.
+ Arrange the ingredients. When filling your slow cooker, put the root vegetables around the bottom and sides of your slow cooker, then place your meat on top.
+ Take notes and experiment. It may take some trial and error to tweak your old favourites but it'll be worth it. Adjust liquids as you go (adding or removing) and keep an eye on cooking times. Take notes as you try new things so you'll always know what worked the best for you. Soon you'll have a recipe you can use anywhere!

| Stovetop & Oven Cooking Times | Slow Cooking on LOW Cooking Times | Slow Cooking on HIGH Cooking Times |
|---|---|---|
| 15–30 mins | 4–6 hours | 1½–2½ hours |
| 45 mins–1 hour | 6½–8 hours | 3–4 hours |
| 1½–2½ hours | 9–12 hours | 4½–6 hours |
| 3–5 hours | 12½–18 hours | 5–7 hours |

# Set 1

Mexican Taco Soup

40 Clove Chicken

Sausages in Brown Onion Gravy

Family Friendly Beef Curry

Deluxe Loaded Potatoes

Spinach and Ricotta Stuffed Rigatoni

Lush Roast Beef and Gravy

# Mexican Taco Soup

This dish is guaranteed to surprise – a thick lush soup with your favourite taco flavours. It's tasty and filling and oh so easy. I make extra so I have leftovers to use the next day because I enjoy it so much. It has a nice mild flavour for even the youngest family members. While you can use canned or frozen corn kernels, I really do recommend them cut off the cob as I have done here, so they keep their sweet crunchy bite throughout the final soup – so good! Serve with a dollop of sour cream and a few corn chips.

Preparation 15 mins • Cook 5 hours • Cooker capacity 6 litres • Serves 8

500 g (1 lb 2 oz) minced (ground) lean beef
1 brown onion, diced
400 g (14 oz) can diced tomatoes
2 x 125 g (4 oz) cans diced red and green capsicum (pepper) (see notes)
3 fresh corn cobs, kernels removed
30 g (1 oz) sachet taco seasoning
4 cups (1 L) chicken stock
2 x 420 g (15 oz) cans mild chilli beans (see notes)
2 cups cooked brown rice (see notes)
300 ml (10 fl oz) sour cream
Corn chips and extra sour cream, to serve

1. Brown the mince and soften the onion in a searing slow cooker for a few minutes with a little spray oil. Use a frying pan if you don't have a searing slow cooker, then transfer.

2. Stir in the tomatoes, capsicum, corn, taco seasoning, stock, chilli beans and cooked rice.

3. Cover and cook on low for 5 hours, stirring in the sour cream for the last 20 minutes of cooking so it heats through.

4. Spoon soup into bowls. Serve topped with a dollop of extra sour cream and a handful of corn chips.

**Notes:** I use canned capsicum as it has a lovely soft consistency, but you could dice ½ a red and ½ a green fresh capsicum if you prefer. You'll find the chilli beans near the baked beans in your supermarket. Alternatively, you can use canned red kidney beans or pinto beans.

For the cooked rice I use the microwave quick-cook cups that cook in 40 seconds each.

# 40 Garlic Clove Chicken

Yes, you read that right – 40 cloves of garlic! As a family we LOVE garlic but it's not half as strong as you may think, I promise! It's amazing and not at all overpowering in taste or smell in the final dish, as it mellows a lot when cooked. I buy a bulk bag of peeled garlic cloves from my local produce store, and some wholesale shops have them too. I freeze the rest until I need them. If you are peeling them yourself you'll need approximately 2 full bulbs of garlic.

**Preparation** 15 mins • **Cook** 5 hours • **Cooker capacity** 5 litres • **Serves** 5

10 chicken thighs (bone in, skin on – not fillets)
2 heaped teaspoons chicken stock powder
1½ tablespoons butter
40 garlic cloves, peeled
½ cup white wine
8–10 sprigs fresh thyme
2 tablespoons chopped fresh parsley
2–3 tablespoons chicken gravy powder or granules, optional

1. Lay the chicken out on a board or dish, skin side up. Season with salt and pepper and sprinkle skin with the stock powder.

2. Melt the butter in a searing slow cooker (or frying pan if you don't have a searing slow cooker).

3. Add the chicken thighs skin side down and sear briefly until lightly browned, for nice colour and maximum flavour.

4. If you used a searing slow cooker simply turn the chicken so it is skin side up and return to slow cooking mode. If you used a frying pan, transfer chicken and buttery pan juices to a slow cooker. Pour in the wine and arrange the garlic cloves around the chicken.

5. Add the thyme and parsley.

6. Cover and cook on LOW for 5 hours.

7. If you do not wish to make gravy, simply remove chicken pieces from cooking liquid and serve with seasonal fresh vegetables. We serve with baby potatoes, steamed carrot, fresh corn on the cob and steamed broccolini.

8. If you wish to make gravy, remove the chicken, cover and set aside to keep warm. Strain the cooking liquid to remove all the solids. Transfer the liquid to a small saucepan and whisk in the gravy powder or granules. Whisk constantly over medium-low heat until thickened to gravy consistency. Serve with the chicken.

# Sausages in Brown Onion Gravy

This is a budget-friendly, easy to prepare and delicious recipe of sausages and gravy – what's not to love! I always try to set aside a serve of leftovers for lunch the next day too as it reheats beautifully.

**Preparation** 10 mins • **Cook** 5 hours • **Cooker capacity** 5 litres • **Serves** 4–6

1 kg (2 lb 3 oz) thin beef sausages
2 brown onions, sliced
½ cup instant gravy powder (see note)
4 cups (1 L) water

1. Add the sausages and onion to the slow cooker bowl.
2. Combine the gravy powder and water until smooth, then pour into the slow cooker.
3. Cover and cook on low for 5 hours.

**Note:** You can use any gravy mix you prefer. If using sachets I would recommend adding at least 3, with appropriate amount of water, as per package instructions.

# Family Friendly Beef Curry

This is a mild curry the whole family can enjoy, but you could add a little more curry powder if you like it hotter! Serve with rice, mashed potato or cauliflower mash to soak up the lush coconut cream sauce.

**Preparation** 15 mins • **Cook** 7 hours • **Cooker capacity** 6 litres • **Serves** 4

1 kg (2 lb 3 oz) blade steak, cubed
1 large brown onion, diced
1 tablespoon minced garlic
2 teaspoons minced ginger
3 teaspoons mild curry powder
½ teaspoon ground turmeric
400 ml (13½ fl oz) can coconut cream
2 teaspoons cornflour (cornstarch)
1 tablespoon soy sauce
1 tablespoon brown sugar (firmly packed)
1–2 tablespoons cornflour (cornstarch), extra, to thicken

1. Place the diced beef and the onion into the slow cooker.

2. Combine all other ingredients well in a jug (except the extra cornflour) and pour over the beef and onion.

3. Cover and cook on low for 6½ hours.

4. Mix the extra cornflour with a little water in a small bowl until smooth. Stir into the mixture in the slow cooker. Cover and cook for a further 30 minutes, to thicken.

# Deluxe Loaded Potatoes

These potatoes are a meal in themselves! Each one is loaded with a delicious creamy chicken mixture and served with its own cheesy sauce.

Preparation 20 mins • Cook 6 hours • Cooker capacity 7 litres • Serves 4

4 large potatoes (see note)
1 large cooked chicken breast (BBQ chicken is ideal),
    shredded then finely chopped
¼ cup spreadable cream cheese
½ small green capsicum (pepper), diced
100 g (3½ oz) diced bacon
⅓ cup grated parmesan
420 g (15 oz) can cream of chicken soup
200 ml (7 fl oz) light sour cream
1 teaspoon cornflour (cornstarch)
½ cup grated parmesan, extra
2 tablespoons chopped fresh chives
salt and pepper to season

1. Cut each potato in half horizontally, so they will be stable and have a wide cut surface.

2. Place halved potatoes into the slow cooker, cut side up.

3. Cover and cook on high by themselves for 2½–3 hours, or until tender enough to be able to scoop without falling apart when handled (I found 2 hours 45 minutes perfect in my slow cooker but this time can vary).

4. Use a large slotted spoon to carefully lift potatoes from slow cooker. Turn the slow cooker off while you prepare next step.

5. Using a tablespoon, scoop out the centre of each potato, leaving about a 1 cm (½ inch) shell. We won't need the scooped out flesh for this recipe so use it in your next potato salad or mash if you like so as not to waste it.

6. In a bowl, combine the chicken, cream cheese, capsicum, bacon and ⅓ cup parmesan. Season with salt and pepper. Divide mixture to fill each potato. It's okay if the filling sits a little high above the potato shell. Carefully place each filled potato into the slow cooker.

7. Mix the soup (no water added), sour cream, cornflour and extra parmesan together well.

8. Pour this sauce into the slow cooker, around and in between each potato. Spoon some of the sauce around the rim of each potato but avoid pouring it over the filling itself.

9. Cover, putting a tea towel (dish towel) under the lid, and cook on low for 3 hours.

10. Use a large slotted spoon to lift the potatoes out of the cooker, fully supported from underneath, and gently place 2 halves on each serving plate.

11. Spoon sauce around and on the rims of each potato. Sprinkle with fresh chives and serve immediately

**Note:** Choose potatoes that are long, so they fit nicely into the slow cooker, and flatter on the wide sides, so that when you cut each potato in half it has a semi-flat surface to sit on.

# Spinach and Ricotta Stuffed Rigatoni

A decadent and delicious vegetarian recipe. This is a great option for your next dinner party that everyone can enjoy! Serve with a fresh green salad on the side and you'll have empty plates all round, as everyone at your table enjoys this meal to the very last bite!

**Preparation** 20 mins • **Cook** 4½ hours • **Cooker capacity** 5 litres • **Serves** 6

125 g (4½ oz) frozen chopped spinach
1 egg
365 g (12¾ oz) smooth ricotta
1 cup grated mozzarella, plus ½ cup extra
½ cup finely grated parmesan, plus ½ cup extra
2 teaspoons minced garlic
1 teaspoon dried Italian herbs
½ teaspoon each salt and cracked black pepper
½ teaspoon onion powder
½ teaspoon garlic powder
3 x 500 g (1 lb 2 oz) jars marinara or Napolitana sauce
200 ml (6¾ fl oz) cooking cream
¼ cup chopped fresh basil
400 g (14 oz) oversized rigatoni (No 321 size)
2 teaspoons chopped fresh parsley, and a little extra to garnish
Shaved parmesan, to serve

1. Place the spinach into a microwave safe bowl with 1–2 tablespoons of water. Microwave on high for 6 minutes, until thawed. Drain well then cool slightly and squeeze out excess liquid, patting with paper towel to soak away any remaining liquid.

2. Add spinach to a large mixing bowl and combine with egg, ricotta, 1 cup mozzarella, ½ cup parmesan, garlic, herbs, salt, pepper, onion and garlic powder. (Reserve the extra mozzarella and parmesan in the fridge for now as you will use them towards the end of cooking time.)

3. In another large bowl combine the jars of sauce with the cooking cream and basil. Add just ⅓ of this mixture to the slow cooker bowl.

4. Spoon the spinach and cheese mixture into a large zip lock bag or other strong plastic bag. Snip off a corner of the bag with scissors and use this as your piping bag to fill each rigatoni with the mixture. One by one, as you fill each pasta piece,

lay it in a single layer on top of the sauce already in your slow cooker. If you find you need a second layer, that is okay.

5. Pour the remaining sauce mixture over the pasta to completely cover it. Pasta not covered in the sauce can be dry and hard so you want it to be coated well.

6. Cover and cook on low for 4 hours or until pasta is tender.

7. Top with the extra mozzarella and parmesan and sprinkle with the parsley.

8. Cook, covered, for an additional 30 minutes. Serve immediately, sprinkled with extra parsley and shaved parmesan.

# Lush Roast Beef and Gravy

I adore a tender slow cooked roast beef. We really enjoy the rich flavours of the chutney and tomato-based gravy and I assure you that you'll want a generous serve of it drizzled over your beef and vegetables too!

**Preparation** 15 mins • **Cook** 6 or 8 hours • **Cooker capacity** 5 litres • **Serves** 6–8

1 brown onion, diced
1.5 kg (3 lb 5 oz) beef roast (blade or topside)
250 g (9 oz) fruit chutney
2 heaped tablespoons tomato paste (concentrated puree)
2 tablespoons gravy powder

1. Spread the onion over the base of the slow cooker bowl and sit the beef on top.
2. Combine the chutney, tomato paste and gravy powder, then spread the mixture over the beef.
3. Cover and cook on low for 6 hours if using 1 kg piece, or 8 hours for 2 kg piece.
4. Remove the beef and allow to rest while you thicken the sauce
5. Reduce the cooking liquid on the searing setting of your slow cooker, or transfer to a saucepan and cook on the stove for about 5 minutes over high heat, stirring constantly, until thickened.
6. Slice the roast beef (I get best results with an electric knife if you have one), then serve with the lush rich gravy generously poured over the beef and vegetables of choice.

# Notes

# Set 1 Shopping List

**MEAT**
500 g (1 lb 2 oz) beef mince
10 x chicken thighs, bone in, skin on
1 kg (2 lb 3 oz) thin beef sausages
1 kg (2 lb 3 oz) blade steak
Beef: 1–2 kg (2 lb 3 oz–4 lb 6 oz) piece
    for roasting
1 large cooked chicken breast (eg from hot
    BBQ chicken)
100 g (3½ oz) diced bacon

**COLD PRODUCTS**
600 ml (20 fl oz) sour cream
1½ tablespoons salted butter
¼ cup spreadable cream cheese
2 cups grated Parmesan cheese
365 g (13 oz) smooth ricotta cheese
1½ cups grated mozzarella cheese
125 g (4½ oz) frozen spinach
1 egg
200 ml (7 fl oz) cooking cream

**FRESH PRODUCE**
5 onions
3 fresh corn cobs
4 large potatoes
½ green capsicum
2 full heads fresh garlic
8–10 sprigs fresh thyme
1 bunch fresh parsley
2 tablespoons fresh chives
3 tablespoons fresh basil

**PANTRY**
400 g (14 oz) can diced tomato
3 x 500 g (1 lb 2 oz) jars of marinara or
    Napolitana sauce
3 tablespoons tomato paste (concentrated
    puree)
250 g (9 oz) fruit chutney
2 x 125 g (4½ oz) cans diced capsicum
30 g (1 oz) sachet taco seasoning
1 litre (2 pt) liquid chicken stock
2 x 420 g (13 oz) can mild chilli beans
420 g (13 oz) can condensed cream of
    chicken soup
Brown rice x 2 cups microwave quick cook
Bag of tortilla/corn chips
3 teaspoons chicken stock powder
½ cup white wine
400 g (14 oz) oversized rigatoni pasta
    (No 321 size)
400 ml (13½ fl oz) can coconut cream
1 tablespoon soy sauce (I like salt reduced)
1 sachet chicken gravy
4 sachets (or one tub) brown gravy (eg roast
    meat or traditional)
2 tablespoons minced ginger (or fresh piece)
1 tablespoon minced garlic (or extra fresh
    garlic)
½ teaspoons turmeric
1 teaspoons dried Italian herbs
½ teaspoons onion powder
½ teaspoons garlic powder
3 teaspoons mild curry powder
1 tablespoon brown sugar
Cornflour
Cracked black pepper
Salt

# Extras

# Set 2

Hearty Chicken and Vegetable Soup with Pasta Spirals

French Cream Chicken

Classic Curried Sausages

Creamy Chicken and Asparagus

Indian-at-Home Beef Mince

Hoisin Pork Bao Buns

Asian Inspired Rack of Lamb

# Hearty Chicken and Vegetable Soup with Pasta Spirals

This is a hearty, belly-filling soup filled with flavour and boosted with vegetable goodness. We serve ours with hot bake-at-home dinner rolls on the side to dunk in the hot soup. If you have home-made chicken stock it's even better, but packaged liquid stock is perfectly okay to keep things nice and easy.

**Preparation 20 mins • Cook 6 hours • Cooker capacity 6 litres • Serves 8**

4 litres (1 gallon) chicken stock
1 kg (2 lb 3 oz) skinless chicken thigh fillets, cut into chunks
2 carrots, finely diced
2 celery stalks, thinly sliced
½ leek, thinly sliced
½ brown onion, diced
2 fresh corn cobs, kernels removed, cores discarded
2 x 50 g (1¾ oz) packets chicken noodle soup mix
⅓ cup dehydrated peas (or 1 cup frozen peas)
½ teaspoon cracked black pepper
2 cups spiral pasta
Crusty bread rolls, to serve

1. Add all the ingredients to the slow cooker, except the pasta.

2. Cover and cook on low for 5 hours 20 minutes.

3. Add the pasta, cover and cook for another 40 minutes or until the pasta is tender.

4. Serve with crusty bread rolls.

# French Cream Chicken

This recipe originally came about while I was trying some low carb eating and I never imagined how popular it would be! It's an ahhhh-mazing creamy chicken dish you'll love – be sure to check the notes section of this recipe for lots of yummy variations! Serve with rice (or cauliflower rice) and steamed greens.

**Preparation** 15 mins • **Cook** 1hr 45 mins • **Cooker capacity** 6 litres • **Serves** 4–6

1 kg (2 lb 3 oz) skinless chicken thigh fillets, diced
225 g (8 oz) block cream cheese, chopped
20 g (¾ oz) French onion soup mix (see notes)
300 ml (10 fl oz) cooking cream
120 g (4½ oz) baby spinach leaves

1. Add a teaspoon of oil to the searing slow cooker or a tablespoon in a frying pan then brown the diced chicken.

2. Add the cream cheese and soup mix. Stir for 2–3 minutes to melt and coat the chicken. Return chicken to slow cooker setting or transfer to slow cooker. Stir in the cooking cream.

3. Cover, putting a tea towel (dish towel) under the lid, and cook on high for 1½ hours.

4. Add the spinach and stir through until wilted.

**Notes:** This uses half a 40 g (1½ oz) packet of French onion soup mix.

The recipe can be easily changed simply by changing the flavour of the cream cheese. For example, I now love a sweet chilli version that I make the same way, but I leave out the French onion soup mix and use sweet chilli flavoured cream cheese. If you can't find this then add ½ cup sweet chilli sauce to your regular cream cheese. You could also cook this with chive and onion cream cheese or apricot cream cheese – so many options!

I've also replaced the baby spinach with semi-dried tomatoes for another yummy version.

# Classic Curried Sausages

This recipe doesn't use the cream base of many curried sausage recipes, and it can be made with low fat sausages to keep it friendly on the waistline but still extra friendly on the tastes buds! Load it up with vegetables for maximum goodness. It's a great recipe for the end of the week to use up vegetables in your crisper, so feel free to swap them for what you have on hand.

**Preparation** 10 mins • **Cook** 6–8 hours • **Cooker capacity** 5 litres • **Serves** 4

500 g (1 lb 2 oz) thin beef or pork sausages
1 large brown onion, diced
4 potatoes, cubed
3 carrots, sliced into chunks
1 cup frozen peas
1 tablespoon curry powder (or extra to taste)
3 cups beef stock
2 tablespoons cornflour (cornstarch)
Steamed rice, to serve

1. Place the sausages into the slow cooker. I put mine in raw, but if you prefer you can par-boil them to remove the skins.
2. Add the remaining ingredients (except the cornflour) and cook on low for 6–8 hours, until the potato is tender.
3. Remove the sausages from the sauce, slice and set aside.
4. Check whether the sauce needs thickening. If you think it does, stir the cornflour with 2 tablespoons water until smooth. Stir into the sauce.
5. Return sausages to the slow cooker. Cover and cook for 10 minutes or until sauce has thickened.
6. Serve with rice.

# Creamy Chicken and Asparagus

The creamy flavours of this recipe pair perfectly with creamy mashed potato. It's filling and delicious! This could also make a lovely pie filling if you like.

**Preparation** 15 mins • **Cook** 4 hours • **Cooker capacity** 5 litres • **Serves** 5

1 kg (2 lb 3 oz) skinless chicken thigh fillets, diced
1 cup button mushrooms, sliced
2 bunches asparagus, trimmed, cut into 3 cm (1 inch) pieces
300 ml (10 fl oz) cooking cream
420 g (15 oz) can condensed cream of asparagus soup
1 teaspoon cracked black pepper
1 teaspoon mustard powder
1 garlic clove, minced
1½ cups grated tasty or cheddar cheese
Steamed white rice or mashed potato, to serve

1. Place the chicken, mushrooms and asparagus into the slow cooker.

2. Combine the remaining ingredients (except the cheese) and add to the slow cooker.

3. Cover and cook on low for 3½ hours.

4. Stir in the cheese, cover and cook for a further 30 minutes.

5. Serve with white rice or creamy mashed potato.

# Indian-at-Home Beef Mince

I love Indian food but I can't often afford to buy it, so making it at home in the slow cooker is the perfect solution! This dish is a little spicy – I'd say medium – so if you prefer it to be milder reduce the korma paste to ¼ cup. We serve this with basmati rice and naan bread and it's amazing!

**Preparation** 10 mins • **Cook** 4 hours • **Cooker capacity** 3.5 litres • **Serves** 4

1 kg (2 lb 3 oz) minced (ground) lean beef (or beef and veal)
1 brown onion, finely diced
⅓ cup mild korma paste
2 tablespoons tomato paste (concentrated puree)
330 ml (11 fl oz) coconut milk

1. Combine all the ingredients in the slow cooker.

2. Cover and cook on low for 4 hours. Season with salt to taste.

# Hoisin Pork Bao Buns

This recipe looks amazing on your plate and would be the perfect show-stopping dish for your next dinner party! The small, fluffy, cloud-like bao buns can be purchased from the frozen section of your regular supermarket and steamed in the microwave in under 2 minutes. While the garnishes take a little time to prepare, the finished dish is totally worth the effort! Perfect to impress your guests!

**Preparation** 45 mins • **Cook** 4 hours • **Cooker capacity** 5 litres
• **Serves** 10 (entrée) or 5 (main)

1 kg (2 lb 3 oz) pork fillets
½ cup hoisin sauce
2 tablespoons soy sauce
2 tablespoons brown sugar
1 tablespoon apple cider vinegar
1 teaspoon Chinese five spice
15–20 bao buns
2 Lebanese cucumbers
2 carrots
4 green onions/scallions/eschallots
1 bunch coriander
Sesame seeds, to serve
Extra hoisin sauce, to serve (mixed with a little water just to reach runny consistency)

1. Place the pork fillets into the slow cooker.
2. Combine the hoisin, soy, sugar, vinegar and five spice and pour over.
3. Cover and cook on low for 4 hours.
4. While the pork cooks, slice the cucumbers into long lengths and then cut these lengths into sticks about the length of the buns.
5. Using a peeler, peel long strips from the carrots, then cut these strips into thin matchsticks, again about the length of the buns.
6. Cut the green onions into pieces about the length of buns. Cut along one side to open up into flat sheets, then cut these into fine ribbon strips.
7. Remove the coriander leaves from stems and roughly chop. Store the vegies and herbs, covered, in the fridge until serving time.
8. When the pork is cooked, shred into large chunks and return to the cooking liquid. The pork will soak up the liquid while you assemble buns.

9. Cook the buns as per packet instructions (mine took 1½ minutes in a microwave, but you can also use a steamer).

10. To assemble, open each bun and add 2 sticks of cucumber and a few carrot strips. Top with the pork and drizzle over a little extra hoisin sauce. Garnish with green onion ribbons, plenty of coriander and a sprinkle of sesame seeds.

11. Serve immediately.

# ⊨— Asian Inspired Rack of Lamb —●

A beautiful twist on the classic roast lamb. I was able to fit this in my 3.5 litre slow cooker but by all means if your rack of lamb is larger it can also be done in a large cooker. We served ours with crispy roast potatoes, pumpkin slices and mushy peas.

**Preparation** 10 mins • **Cook** 5 hours • **Cooker capacity** 3.5 litres • **Serves** 4

1 rack of lamb (see note)
½ cup hoisin sauce
2 garlic cloves, minced
1 tablespoon sesame oil
1 tablespoon soy sauce
1 tablespoon brown sugar
1 tablespoon rice wine vinegar

1. Place the lamb rack into the slow cooker, bone side up.

2. Combine all the other ingredients and pour over the lamb.

3. Cover and cook on low for 5 hours, basting with the pan juices occasionally during cooking for rich colour and flavour.

4. Rest for 10 minutes before serving.

**Note:** Choose a rack that allows 2–3 cutlets per person.

# Notes

# Set 2 Shopping List

**MEAT**
3 kg (6 lb 9 oz) skinless chicken thigh fillets
500 g (1 lb 2 oz) thin sausages (beef or pork)
1 kg (2 lb 3 oz) lean beef mince (or beef and
    veal mix)
1 kg (2 lb 3 oz) pork fillet (or 2 x 500 g
    [1 lb 2 oz] pieces)
1 rack of lamb (approx. 2–3 cutlets per
    person)

**COLD PRODUCTS**
225 g (8 oz) block Philadelphia cream cheese
600 ml (10 fl oz) cooking cream
1 cup frozen peas (or 2 cups if not using
    dehydrated peas below)
1½ cups grated tasty or cheddar cheese
15–20 bao buns (usually in the supermarket
    freezer section)

**FRESH PRODUCE**
7 carrots
4 potatoes
2 celery sticks
3 onions
½ leek
2 fresh corn cobs
120 g (4½ oz) baby spinach leaves
2 bunches asparagus
1 cup button mushrooms
2 medium Lebanese cucumbers
4 green onions/scallions/eschalots
Bunch of fresh coriander

**PANTRY**
4 litres (8½ pt) liquid chicken stock
750 ml (26 fl oz) liquid beef stock
2 x 50 g (1¾ oz) packets dry chicken noodle
    soup mix
1 sachet dry French onion soup mix
420 g (13 oz) condensed cream of asparagus
    soup
⅓ cup dehydrated peas (or 1 cup frozen
    peas)
2 cups spiral pasta
1 tablespoon mild curry powder
1 teaspoons mustard powder
3 teaspoons minced garlic (or 3 cloves fresh)
⅓ cup mild korma paste
2 tablespoons tomato paste (concentrated
    puree)
330 ml (11 fl oz) coconut milk
1 cup hoisin sauce + extra to serve
3 tablespoons soy sauce (I like salt reduced)
3 tablespoons brown sugar
1 teaspoon 5 spice powder
Sesame seeds
1 tablespoon sesame oil
1 tablespoon rice wine vinegar
1 tablespoon apple cider vinegar
(these 2 vinegars can both substitute for
    each other if you don't want to purchase
    both kinds)
Cornflour
Cracked pepper
Salt

# Extras

_____

_____

_____

_____

_____

_____

_____

_____

_____

_____

_____

_____

_____

_____

_____

_____

_____

_____

_____

# Set 3

Miso Ramen Soup

Lamb Tagine

Sausage and Chorizo Hotpot

Tomato and Spinach Bocconcini Mince

Stuffing-mix Meatballs with a Cranberry BBQ Sauce

Nanny's Braised Steak

Dusted Roast Pork

# Miso Ramen Soup

This was the first time I tried cooking a Japanese recipe. It was inspired by a miso soup I saw being cooked on a UK TV fitness show, and safe to say – I was thrilled with the outcome 😊. I began with a litre of homemade chicken stock for maximum flavour. If you can't make it, purchase the best quality stock you can afford to make this dish taste the absolute best. If purchasing I find liquids stocks have a better flavour than powder or stock cubes.

**Preparation** 20 mins • **Cook** 4½ hours • **Cooker capacity**: 6 litres • **Serves** 2 large or 4 small

> 4 cups chicken stock (see note)
> 20 g dried porcini mushrooms (see note)
> 1 whole garlic bulb
> 1 bunch green onions/scallions/eschallots, trimmed
> 4 star anise
> 3 cm (1 inch) piece ginger, roughly sliced
> 4 skinless chicken thigh fillets, trimmed
> 1 tablespoon salt-reduced soy sauce
> 1 tablespoon white miso paste (in the Asian section at the supermarket)
> 20 g dried shiitake mushrooms (see note)
> 125 g (2 squares/cakes) dried noodles
> 60 g (2 oz) baby spinach leaves
> 1 hard-boiled (or medium-boiled) egg per serve, halved
> Sliced red chilli, to garnish (optional)

1. Pour the chicken stock (room or fridge temperature, not hot) into the slow cooker and add the porcini mushrooms.

2. Roughly flatten the garlic cloves with the side of a large knife and remove the skin. Add to the slow cooker. (This will be removed later when the soup is strained so don't be overly concerned if a little skin goes in with them.)

3. Cut the white and pale green ends from the green onions and add to the slow cooker. Slice and reserve approximately 1 cup of the darker green ends and place them in the fridge for now; you'll use them later for garnishing the soup.

4. Add the star anise, ginger and whole chicken fillets to the slow cooker.

5. Cover and cook on HIGH for 3 hours.

6. Remove the chicken from the soup and transfer to a cutting board. Use a large slotted spoon to remove the solids from the soup, and discard.

7. Shred the chicken and return to the soup. Stir in the soy sauce, miso paste and dried shiitake mushrooms.

8. Cover and cook on LOW for 1 hour.

9. Add the dried noodles and spinach leaves and cook for a further 30 minutes or until the noodles are soft and the spinach wilted.

10. Divide between 2 large serving bowls (or 4 small bowls).

11. Top with the sliced green onions and the eggs (2 halves per bowl). If you like a little extra heat you can also scatter with chilli.

**Notes:** Use the BEST quality chicken stock you can get or, better still, make your own. You'll find dried porcini and shitake mushrooms in the fresh veggie section at the supermarket.

# Lamb Tagine

A tagine usually refers to a slow-simmered stew traditionally cooked in a covered earthenware pot with a wide base and tall narrow lid. This cooking vessel maintains a moist cooking environment as the steam rises and condensation forms in the lid then trickles back into the dish. Just like our slow cookers! This is why a tagine is perfect for slow cooking. This tagine features the flavour of lamb and spices with the goodness of chickpeas and sweet potato to make it filling, nutritious and delicious! Serve with your choice of couscous, rice or bread.

**Preparation** 20 mins • **Cook** 7 hours • **Cooker capacity** 3.5 litres • **Serves** 4

500 g (1 lb 2 oz) diced lamb
400 g (14 oz) can diced tomatoes
420 g (15 oz) can chickpeas, drained and rinsed
1 small brown onion, diced
½ large orange sweet potato, diced
½ red capsicum (pepper), diced
1 garlic clove
80 g (3 oz) dried apricots, cut into quarters
1 teaspoon ground cumin
1 teaspoon ground coriander
1 teaspoon ground cinnamon
1 teaspoon ground paprika
1 teaspoon ground turmeric
½ teaspoon ground ginger
1 tablespoon honey
1 teaspoon salt
½ teaspoon cracked black pepper
Fresh coriander and slivered almonds, to serve

1. Combine all the ingredients in the slow cooker.

2. Cover and cook on low for 7 hours.

3. Divide among bowls and garnish with coriander and slivered almonds. Serve with your preferred side dish.

# Sausage and Chorizo Hotpot

A pot full of yum! Serve this hearty hotpot with a side of creamy mashed potato for the whole family to enjoy.

**Preparation** 10 mins • **Cook** 6 hours • **Cooker capacity** 5 litres • **Serves** 5

10 thin beef sausages
1 chorizo sausage, about 125 g (4½ oz)
1 small brown onion, diced
2 tablespoons tomato paste (concentrated puree)
400 g (14 oz) can diced tomatoes
555 g (1 lb 5 oz) can baked beans
1½ teaspoons smoked paprika
1 teaspoon cracked black pepper
1 teaspoon mixed dried herbs
2 garlic cloves, minced
1 tablespoon Worcestershire sauce
6 cherry tomatoes, cut into quarters

1. Using kitchen scissors, chop the raw sausages into bite-sized pieces and place into the slow cooker.

2. Halve the chorizo lengthways then thinly slice and add to the slow cooker.

3. Add all the other ingredients and mix gently to combine.

4. Cover and cook on low for 6 hours.

# Tomato and Spinach Bocconcini Mince

If you want a dish that, when served, makes people say 'wow that looks amazing!' – this is your dish! With the vibrant reds, melted cheesy balls and fresh green garnish, it's an absolute feast for your eyes ☺. Luckily the taste is just as impressive! Serve with a vibrant green side salad and some al dente rigatoni pasta. A sure hit for any dinner, be it entertaining others or just treating your family, it will bring you great feedback from all!

Preparation 15 mins • Cook 4 hours • Cooker capacity 6 litres • Serves 5

1 leek (white part only)
1 kg (2 lb 3 oz) minced (ground) lean beef
4 garlic cloves, minced
500 ml (17 fl oz) passata (pureed tomato)
60 g (2 oz) baby spinach leaves
2 teaspoons dried basil
2 teaspoons dried oregano
100 ml (3½ fl oz) cooking cream
200 g (7 oz) grape (or cherry) tomatoes, halved
220 g (7¾ oz) tub cherry bocconcini
Fresh basil leaves, to garnish

1. Halve the leek lengthways, slice thinly then finely chop. Add to the slow cooker with the mince.

2. Add the garlic, passata, spinach leaves and dried herbs.

3. Cover and cook on low for 2½ hours.

4. Stir through the cooking cream and tomatoes (reserve a few tomato halves for garnish).

5. Cover and cook for another 1 hour, then drop the bocconcini on top of mixture, spaced apart.

6. Cover and cook for a further 30 minutes or until the cheese begins to melt.

7. Serve scattered with fresh basil leaves and remaining tomatoes.

# Stuffing-mix Meatballs with a BBQ Cranberry Sauce

Our family LOVE meatballs – kids never turn down a tasty meatball so we cook them so many different ways. However, over Christmas I got to thinking about cranberry sauce and how amazing it would be with meatballs. The use of a prepared stuffing mix replaces the need for breadcrumbs in the meatballs and the flavour it brings is AMAZING! This makes around 60 small meatballs, but the quantity can be halved if you prefer. Great for entertaining, or simply served with mash, rice or hot chips for an easy tasty dinner the whole family will enjoy!

**Preparation** 30 mins + 1 hour chilling • **Cook** 4 hours • **Cooker capacity** 6 litres • Makes 60

**MEATBALLS**
1 kg (2 lb 3 oz) minced (ground) pork and veal (see note)
1 small brown onion, finely diced
2 eggs
200 g (7 oz) box seasoned stuffing mix
½ cup water
½ cup milk
½ teaspoon garlic powder

**SAUCE**
275 g (10 oz) jar jellied cranberry sauce
250 ml (9 fl oz) BBQ sauce
1 tablespoon brown sugar

**GARNISH**
Finely sliced green onions/scallions/eschallots and sesame seeds (optional)

1. Combine all the meatball ingredients in a large mixing bowl. Using clean hands (or I like to wear disposable kitchen gloves), roll into small meatballs (no bigger than a table tennis ball). You should get around 60 from this mixture.

2. Place meatballs into a dish or on a large plate as you roll. Once all rolled, cover and refrigerate for an hour before cooking.

3. When it's time to cook, gently place meatballs into slow cooker. It's okay if they overlap.

4. Combine the sauce ingredients and pour over the meatballs.

5. Cover and cook on low for 4 hours. DO NOT STIR the meatballs for at least the first 3 hours of cooking. After this time they will be firmer and you can then gently move them around, away from each other if any are slightly stuck, or to alternate top layer with bottom layer to make sure they are coated in the sauce. The key to keeping the meatballs perfectly intact is leaving them alone for the first few hours.

6. Use a slotted spoon to gently transfer the meatballs to a serving plate. Cover to keep warm. Heat the sauce in a saucepan over high heat on the stove, stirring constantly for 5–10 minutes or until reduced and thickened slightly. Spoon the sauce over the meatballs and garnish with the green onions and sesame seeds, if using.

**Note:** Pork and veal mince is usually sold as a mixture, but if you can't find it just use 500 g (1 lb 2 oz) of each.

# Nanny's Braised Steak

When I was a little girl my mum cooked the most amazing braised steak recipe, and it was always one of my favourite meals growing up. My mother passed away before I had my children so while they never got to meet her, they know of her as 'Nanny in the stars'. When I created this recipe based on her handwritten recipe in an old recipe folder, we of course named it after her in her honour. Always remembered Mum xx.

**Preparation 15 mins • Cook 5 hours • Cooker capacity 5 litres • Serves 4**

¼ cup mild American mustard (from a squeezy bottle)
¼ cup brown sugar
1 kg (2 lb 3 oz) oyster blade steak (or any affordable casserole-style steak)
2 heaped tablespoons plain (all-purpose) flour
1 large brown onion, thinly sliced
½ cup tomato sauce (ketchup) (I use low-sugar but you can use regular)
1½ tablespoons soy sauce (I use reduced-salt but you can use regular)
Steamed veggies and mash, to serve

1. Place the mustard and sugar into a large plastic bag.

2. Add the steak and toss and rub around to coat the steaks with the mustard and sugar.

3. Place the flour into a second large plastic bag and season with salt and pepper.

4. Tip steak from the first bag into the second bag and toss around to dust the steaks with the seasoned flour.

5. Remove the steak from the bag and lay it in the slow cooker, in a single layer if possible.

6. Top with the onion.

7. Combine the sauces and pour over the steak and onion.

8. Cover and cook on LOW for 5 hours.

9. Serve steak with vegetables and mash, and pour over the lush gravy.

**Notes:** You don't need to add any water to this dish, but you can add ½ cup water if you prefer it more saucy (you really don't need it though).

# Dusted Roast Pork

This simple roast is all about flavour and nothing about complicated effort. It will take only minutes to prepare your meal and the smells all day while it cooks will be amazing! Slice or pull the pork and serve with assorted roast vegetables, or mash and steamed vegetables. You can also add a gravy made from pan juices.

**Preparation** 15 mins • **Cook** 9 hours • **Cooker capacity** 6 litres • **Serves** 6

2 kg (4 lb 6 oz) boneless pork shoulder roast
40 g (1½ oz) sachet traditional or roast gravy powder
1 teaspoon dried rosemary
1 teaspoon smoked paprika
½ teaspoon cracked black pepper
½ teaspoon garlic salt
¼ teaspoon salt

1. Remove any netting from the pork and place fat-side-down into the slow cooker.

2. Combine all the other ingredients and sprinkle over the pork.

3. Cover and cook on low for 9 hours.

4. Carefully remove the pork from the slow cooker – it will be very tender.

5. Remove and discard the fat layer. Cut the pork into thick slices or shred or pull the meat apart.

6. Transfer the pan juices to a saucepan and cook on the stovetop for a few minutes, stirring, to reduce and thicken.

# Notes

# Set 3 Shopping List

**MEAT**
4 skinless chicken thigh fillets
500 g (1 lb 2 oz) diced lamb
10 thin beef sausages
1 kg (2 lb 3 oz) lean beef mince
1 kg (2 lb 3 oz) mixed pork and veal mince
1 kg (2 lb 3 oz) oyster blade steak (or other casserole style steak)
2 kg (4 lb 6 oz) boneless pork shoulder roast

**COLD PRODUCTS**
6 eggs
1 chorizo sausage (approx 125 g [4½ oz])
100 ml (3½ fl oz) cooking cream
1 x 220 g (8 oz) tub of cherry sized bocconcini
½ cup milk

**FRESH PRODUCE**
20 g (¾ oz) dried porcini mushrooms
20 g (¾ oz) dried shitake mushrooms
1 bunch green onions/scallions/eschallots
1 head fresh garlic
1 inch piece fresh ginger
120 g (4½ oz) baby spinach leaves
4 onions
1 leek
6 cherry tomatoes
1 x 200 g (7 oz) punnet grape tomatoes, sliced in half (or extra cherry tomatoes)
½ large orange sweet potato
½ red capsicum
Fresh basil leaves
Optional garnishes: fresh coriander, 1 red chilli

**PANTRY**
1 litre (2 pt) good quality liquid chicken stock
2 x 400 g (14 oz) can crushed/diced tomatoes
2 tablespoons tomato paste (concentrated puree)
1 x 420 g (13 oz) can chickpeas

1 x 555 g (1¾ oz) can baked beans
200 g (7 oz) box dry seasoned stuffing mix
4 dried star anise
3 tablespoons soy sauce (I like salt reduced)
1 tablespoon white miso paste (in Asian section)
125 g (4½ oz/2 squares/cakes) dry noodles (long-life shelf version not fresh)
80 g (2¾ oz) dried apricots
1 teaspoon ground cumin
1 teaspoon ground coriander seeds
1 teaspoon cinnamon
3½ teaspoons paprika
1 teaspoon turmeric
2 teaspoons dried basil
2 teaspoons dried oregano
½ teaspoons garlic powder
1 teaspoon dried rosemary
½ teaspoon minced ginger (or extra fresh)
1 teaspoon mixed dried herbs
½ teaspoons garlic salt
9 cloves minced garlic (or extra head fresh)
1 tablespoon Worcestershire sauce
1 x 275 g (10 oz) jar jellied cranberry sauce
250 ml (9 fl oz) BBQ sauce
½ cup tomato sauce
3 tablespoons mild yellow mustard (I like American style)
⅓ cup brown sugar
1 tablespoon honey
3 tablespoons plain flour
500 g (1 lb 2 oz) passata (pureed tomato)
1 x 40 g (1½ oz) sachet traditional/roast gravy powder
Optional garnish: slivered almonds
Cornflour
Cracked black pepper
Salt

# Extras

_____

_____

_____

_____

_____

_____

_____

_____

_____

_____

_____

_____

_____

_____

_____

_____

_____

_____

_____

# Set 4

Seafood Chowder

Japanese Golden Curry Chicken

Hearty Beef and Vegetable Casserole

Hunters Chicken

Mediterranean Medley with Penne Pasta

Meatballs and Linguine in Creamy Tomato Sauce

Red Wine Roast Beef

# Seafood Chowder

It's not every day most of us can afford seafood, so when you do indulge, you want it to wow! This not only tastes great, it looks amazing too! I use a marinara mix that includes raw prawns, fish, mussels and calamari that you can buy from your supermarket deli seafood counter. Serve with a stone-baked Turkish pide loaf, or other crusty bread or breadstick, cut into thick slices and buttered.

**Preparation** 20 mins • **Cook** 4 hours 45 mins • **Cooker capacity** 5 litres • **Serves** 6

1 kg (2 lb 3 oz) potatoes, cubed
3 carrots, sliced
3 celery stalks, sliced
3 garlic cloves, minced
2 teaspoons cracked black pepper
1 tablespoon chopped fresh parsley
2 tablespoons chopped fresh chives, plus 1 tablespoon, extra
2 cups (500 ml) fish stock (or chicken stock if you can't get fish)
2 fresh corn cobs
750 g (1 lb 11 oz) marinara seafood mix
300 ml (10 fl oz) cooking cream
1 teaspoon cornflour (cornstarch)
Extra chopped fresh chives, to garnish
Crusty buttered bread, to serve

1. Combine the potatoes, carrot, celery, garlic, pepper, parsley, 2 tablespoons chives and the fish stock in the slow cooker.

2. Cover and cook on high for 4 hours.

3. Use a stick blender to blend the soup to a smooth consistency.

4. Cut the kernels from the corn cobs and add to the soup, along with the marinara mix.

5. Cook, covered, for 30 minutes. At the end of this time the seafood should be almost cooked.

6. Combine the cooking cream with the cornflour and gently stir into the soup, along with the remaining 1 tablespoon of fresh chives, taking care not to break up the fish chunks.

7. Cover and cook a further 15 minutes, to heat the cream through and thicken slightly.

8. Garnish and serve with buttered crusty bread.

# Japanese Golden Curry Chicken

I've long been curious about the Japanese curry roux cubes so, naturally, I had to slow cook with them. You'll find them in the Asian foods section of your supermarket, and they usually come in hot, medium and mild. For this recipe we chose mild and it was perfect for even the youngest members of the family – full of flavour but no heat. If you like a bit more bite choose the hotter variety.

**Preparation** 15 mins • **Cook** 5 hours • **Cooker capacity** 5 litres • **Serves** 5

92g (3 oz) box Japanese curry cubes (5 roux cubes)
125 ml (4½ fl oz) boiling water
1 large brown onion, cut into thin wedges
150 g (5¼ oz) green beans, trimmed and cut into pieces
1 kg (2 lb 3 oz) skinless chicken thigh fillets, roughly chopped
60 g (2 oz) baby spinach leaves
1 teaspoon cornflour (cornstarch)
200 ml (7 fl oz) coconut cream

1. Chop the curry cubes and soak in the boiling water.

2. Place the onion, beans, chicken and spinach into the slow cooker.

3. Stir the cornflour into the coconut cream then whisk into the curry and water mixture. Pour into the slow cooker and stir gently to combine.

4. Cover and cook on low for 5 hours, stirring occasionally to help disperse the curry sauce.

**Note:** We love this served with sweet potato mash and steamed baby asparagus and broccolini. You could also serve with rice.

# Hearty Beef and Vegetable Casserole

You can vary the vegetables in this recipe to use whatever you have on hand, so this is a great 'empty out the vegetable crisper at the end of the week' type of recipe. This big hearty casserole fills a 6 litre slow cooker to the top, hence the long and high cooking time to achieve tender results. You could also cook on low all day (I'd estimate about 10 hours at least, so it's a great option for working families cooking from morning until home time). Leftovers freeze well too!

**Preparation** 20 mins • **Cook** 7 hours • **Cooker capacity** 6 litres • **Serves** 8

2 large potatoes, cut into large bite-sized chunks
3 carrots, sliced
1 sweet potato, cut into large bite-sized chunks
¼ butternut pumpkin, cut into large bite-sized chunks
1 large brown onion, diced
200 g (7 oz) green beans, chopped
1 cup frozen green peas
400 g (14 oz) can diced tomatoes
420 g (15 oz) can condensed tomato soup
150 g (5¼ oz) fruit chutney
1 tablespoon Worcestershire sauce
1 teaspoon curry powder
1 teaspoon Vegemite
2 teaspoons plain (all-purpose) flour
1–1.5 kg (2 lb 3 oz–3 lb 5 oz) chuck steak, diced (or any affordable casserole-style steak)
Buttered crusty bread, to serve

1. Combine all the vegetables except the tomatoes in the slow cooker.

2. Place the tomatoes, soup, chutney, sauce, curry powder and Vegemite in a bowl. Mix well and set aside.

3. Put the flour into a large freezer bag and season with salt and pepper. Add the diced beef and toss to coat. Add the beef to the slow cooker on top of the vegetables.

4. Pour over the tomato mixture and stir to combine.

5. Cover and cook on high for 7 hours (see the notes in the recipe introduction).

6. Serve with buttered crusty bread to mop up the delicious sauce.

# Hunter's Chicken

Hunter's chicken is a popular recipe the world over and I've seen everyone including the English, Italians, Americans and French claim it as their own! Put simply, it's chicken wrapped in bacon, served with a BBQ-style sauce and topped with cheese. What's not to love about that! I like to give the sauce an extra depth of flavour with a little seeded mustard and you can of course use your own home-made BBQ sauce if you prefer. We also stuff the breast with cheese – because it's amazing!

**Preparation** 25 mins • **Cook** 2 hours 40 mins **Cooker capacity** 6 litres • **Serves** 4

4 chicken breast fillets
100 g (3½ oz) cheddar cheese, cut into 4 finger-sized sticks
8 rashers streaky bacon
1 cup BBQ sauce
2 teaspoons wholegrain mustard
4 tablespoons finely grated parmesan
1 tablespoon cornflour (cornstarch)

1. Lay the chicken on a cutting board and at the thickest part of each breast, cut a small pocket. Push a cheese stick into each pocket. Push chicken closed again.

2. Wrap each breast with two rashers of streaky bacon. I secure the bacon simply by putting the join underneath the chicken, but you may prefer to secure it with a toothpick.

3. Place the wrapped chicken breasts into the slow cooker bowl.

4. Combine the BBQ sauce and mustard and pour over the chicken.

5. Cover, putting a tea towel (dish towel) under the lid, and cook on high for 2½ hours.

6. Transfer the chicken to a plate and cover to keep warm while you prepare the sauce.

7. Transfer the cooking liquid to a small saucepan on the stovetop (or use a searing slow cooker). Mix the cornflour with 2 tablespoons water until smooth, and stir the mixture into the cooking liquid. Cook over high heat, stirring, for 5–10 minutes, until reduced and thickened.

8. Place the chicken onto serving plates, spoon sauce over then top each serve with 1 tablespoon of parmesan.

**Note:** We've had this served with creamy potato and chive mash, fresh steamed corn cobs and broccolini. It's also great with chunky-cut potato chips and salad or slaw.

# Mediterranean Medley with Penne Pasta

This large pasta dish is absolutely jam-packed with flavour. It makes a large amount, so whatever you don't finish for dinner is lovely packaged up to take to work or school the next day for lunches – two meals taken care of in one!

**Preparation** 20 mins • **Cook** 3½ hours • **Cooker capacity** 6 litres • **Serves** 8

1 tablespoon olive oil
2 chorizo sausages, halved lengthways and thinly sliced
200 g (7 oz) rindless middle bacon, diced
1 large red onion, diced
2–3 garlic cloves, minced
3 cups passata (pureed tomato sauce)
½ eggplant, cut into small cubes
½ cup marinated mushrooms (from deli or a jar)
200 g (7 oz) cherry tomatoes
400 g (14 oz) penne
1 large green capsicum (pepper), thinly sliced
2 handfuls baby spinach
50 g (1¾ oz) shaved parmesan, to serve

1. Heat the olive oil in a frying pan over medium heat (or use a searing slow cooker). Sauté the chorizo, bacon, onion and garlic for about 5 minutes, until soft.

2. Place the passata, eggplant, mushrooms and cherry tomatoes into the slow cooker, then add the sautéed mixture, stirring to combine.

3. Cover and cook for 3 hours on low.

4. Add the penne to a large saucepan of boiling water and cook for ten minutes to al dente only, still slightly firm. Drain, then add the pasta to the slow cooker, stirring through gently so as not to break the tomatoes. Cover and cook for a further 20 minutes.

5. Stir in the green capsicum and spinach and cook, covered, for another 10 minutes.

6. Divide among plates and top with shaved parmesan.

# Meatballs and Linguine in Creamy Tomato Sauce

These delicious, juicy, home-made meatballs will be a hit with the whole family. Serve on linguine with a scattering of parmesan cheese and add a side of garlic bread if you wish. Leftovers can be frozen. Alternatively, you could serve them the next day as meatballs subs for a whole new meal!

**Preparation** 30 mins • **Cook** 5 hours 15 mins • **Cooker capacity** 5 litres • **Serves** 6

500 g (1 lb 2 oz) linguine
Finely grated parmesan, to serve

**MEATBALLS**
500 g (1 lb 2 oz) minced (ground) lean beef
500 g (1 lb 2 oz) sausage mince
½ cup packaged dried breadcrumbs
½ cup finely grated parmesan
1 egg
2 tablespoons milk
1 teaspoon dried parsley
1 teaspoon dried oregano
2 garlic cloves, minced

**SAUCE**
700 g bottle passata (pureed tomato sauce)
2 teaspoons beef stock powder
1 teaspoon cracked black pepper
3 garlic cloves, minced
Handful fresh basil leaves, chopped
125 ml (4½ fl oz) cooking cream

1. Place the sauce ingredients (except cream) into the slow cooker and stir to combine.
2. Put all the meatball ingredients into a large bowl, and using your hands work the mixture to combine well. I like to wear disposable gloves for this to make it easy and mess-free.
3. Roll mixture into approximately 30 medium meatballs. Add them to the slow cooker one by one as you go.
4. Cover and cook on low for 5 hours. Do NOT stir for the first 3–4 hours at all. This will keep them firm and intact, and none will break apart. After this they can be gently stirred if you need to.

5. Add the cooking cream and stir gently to mix through. Cover and cook for a further 15 minutes to ensure the cream heats through.

6. Just before the meatballs and sauce are ready, cook the linguine in a large pan of salted boiling water until al dente. Drain. Serve meatballs and sauce over the cooked linguine and garnish with cheese.

**Notes:** Passata is a thick tomato puree. It's different from canned tomatoes or pasta sauce. You'll find it in the same section of the supermarket.

Sausage mince can be purchased in your supermarket butcher department. It is usually sold in rolls of 500 g (1 lb 2 oz).

You could make your own breadcrumbs if you prefer, but they need to be quite fine.

Use fresh basil and garlic for best flavour.

Lean beef mince balances with the sausage mince well, and avoids the need to remove excess fat from the sauce.

# Red Wine Roast Beef

This roast beef will absolutely melt in your mouth. Pair it with traditional roast vegetables if you wish, but we prefer it with mashed potato and chives and assorted steamed veggies like carrot sticks and broccolini – and that gravy, oh that gravy! If you prefer to use non-alcoholic wine you certainly can. This is a great recipe that you can put on early in the morning and leave completely alone all day, great for a long work day or a busy weekend!

**Preparation** 10 mins • **Cook** 8 hours • **Cooker capacity** 6 litres • **Serves** 6

1 brown onion, roughly chopped
1 carrot, roughly chopped (no need to peel)
2 celery stalks, roughly chopped
3 sprigs fresh rosemary (or 1 tablespoon dried)
2 bay leaves
1.5 kg (3 lb 5 oz) beef blade roast
1 cup red wine (I use cabernet merlot)
½ cup beef stock
2 tablespoons tomato paste (concentrated puree)
1 tablespoon Worcestershire sauce
2 teaspoons sugar
Gravy powder, as needed (see step 5)
Vegetables of your choice, to serve

1. Place the vegetables, rosemary and bay leaves in the base of the slow cooker. Sit the beef on top of vegetables.

2. Combine the wine, beef stock, tomato paste, sauce and sugar and pour over the beef.

3. Cover and cook on low for 8 hours.

4. Remove beef from slow cooker, cover to keep warm and leave to rest while you make the gravy.

5. Strain the solids from the liquid in the slow cooker. Discard the solids and reserve the liquid. Make gravy as directed on the packet, but replace half the usual gravy water with half the cooking liquid, for extra flavour.

6. Carve the meat, serve with your vegetables of choice, and pour over the delicious gravy.

**Note:** Leftover roast beef slices make great sandwich fillings for lunch the following day!

# Notes

_____

_____

_____

_____

_____

_____

_____

_____

_____

_____

_____

_____

_____

_____

_____

_____

# Set 4 Shopping List

**MEAT**
750 g (1 lb 11 oz) marinara seafood mix
1 kg (2 lb 3 oz) chicken thigh fillets
1–1.5 kg (2 lb 3 oz–3 lb 5 oz) diced chuck
    steak or similar casserole beef
4 medium skinless chicken breasts
500 g (1 lb 2 oz) lean beef mince
500 g (1 lb 2 oz) sausage mince
1.5 kg (3 lb 5 oz) piece beef for roasting,
    eg blade roast
8 rashers streaky bacon
200 g (7 oz) rindless middle bacon
2 chorizo sausage (approx. 250 g [9 oz])

**COLD PRODUCTS**
425 ml (14½ fl oz) cooking cream
1 cup frozen peas
100 g (3½ oz) block cheddar cheese
2 cups grated Parmesan cheese
1 egg
2 tablespoons milk

**FRESH PRODUCE**
1 kg (2 lb 3 oz) washed potatoes + 2 extra,
    large
8 carrots
3 brown onions
1 red onion
350 g (1¾ oz) green beans
1 sweet potato
5 celery stalks
¼ butternut pumpkin
2 fresh corn cobs
120 g (4½ oz) baby spinach leaves
1 large green capsicum
½ eggplant
1 punnet cherry tomatoes
11 cloves garlic (or 1 full bulb)
1 tablespoon fresh parsley
3 tablespoons fresh chives + extra to garnish
3 sprigs fresh rosemary (or 1 tablespoon
    dried)
Handful of fresh basil leaves

**PANTRY**
500 ml (17 fl oz) fish stock (or chicken stock
    if you can't get fish)
1 x 92 g (3¼ oz) box Japanese curry mix
    (5 roux cubes)
1 sachet roast meat gravy
200 ml (7 fl oz) coconut cream
1 x 400 g (14 oz) diced/crushed tomatoes
1 x 420 g (13 oz) can condensed tomato
    soup
500 g (1 lb 2 oz) linguine
400 g (14 oz) penne
150 g (5½ oz) fruit chutney
1 teaspoon mild curry powder
1 teaspoons dried parsley
1 teaspoons dried oregano
3 teaspoons beef stock powder
2 tablespoons Worcestershire sauce
1 teaspoon vegemite
2 teaspoons plain flour
1 cup BBQ sauce
2 teaspoons wholegrain seeded mustard
1 tablespoon olive oil
2 x 750 g (1 lb 11 oz) bottle passata
½ cup marinated mushrooms (in jars near
    pickles section)
½ cup packaged dried breadcrumbs
2 bay leaves
1 cup red wine
2 tablespoons tomato paste (concentrated
    puree)
2 teaspoons sugar
Cornflour
Cracked black pepper
Salt

# Extras

_____

_____

_____

_____

_____

_____

_____

_____

_____

_____

_____

_____

_____

_____

_____

_____

_____

_____

_____

# Set 5

Fast 'n' Easy Chicken Soup

Buffalo Chicken Meatballs

Saucy Sweet Pork Steaks

Spaghetti Bolognaise

Chicken and Leek Pie

Shredded Beef Ragu

Roast Lamb with Obsession Sauce

# ⊫— Fast 'n' Easy Chicken Soup —•

This recipe is based on a stovetop soup my mother always cooked when I was little. The smell of it cooking when I returned home from school was always a sign of a great dinner to come! This recipe is designed to be fast and easy to get cooking. It can then be left alone all day to do its thing until you are ready for your 'winner, winner, chicken soup dinner!' Leftovers are great to freeze too. It's a real soup for the soul.

**Preparation 10 mins • Cook 8 hours • Cooker capacity 6 litres • Serves 8**

2 kg (4 lb 6 oz) chicken drumsticks (see note)
500 g (1 lb 2 oz) frozen diced vegetables
2 brown onions, diced
40 g (1½ oz) packet chicken noodle soup mix
¼ cup good-quality chicken stock powder
Crusty bread rolls, to serve

1. Combine all the ingredients in the slow cooker. Fill with water to about 6 cm (2 inches) below the top of the inner cooking bowl.

2. Cover and cook on low for 8 hours.

3. Take the chicken out. Pull the meat from the bones in shreds, then return the meat to the soup. Stir to combine.

4. Serve with crusty bread rolls

**Notes:** While you can use other cuts of chicken, such as wings, I find the drumsticks the easiest to debone. I also prefer skin-on chicken pieces as I find breast fillets can dry out too much. If you really prefer boneless pieces I would suggest thigh fillets over breast fillets.

# Buffalo Chicken Meatballs

What's a mum to do? My teenager begged me to cook 'Buffalo chicken', as he had it in his mind that he would really love the sauce after seeing it on an ad (ha-ha kids huh!?). But I didn't have any chicken wings, so it became.... Buffalo chicken meatballs! Oh me oh my, they didn't disappoint! I drizzled ours with garlic aioli but you could swap that out for ranch dressing if you like, or even a blue cheese dressing (I'm a realist – my kids would leave home if I put blue cheese anything anywhere near their plates!).

Preparation 20 mins • Cook 3½ hours • Cooker capacity: 6 litres • Serves 4

400 ml (13½ fl oz) Buffalo wing sauce
3–4 tablespoons garlic aioli dressing (or ranch dressing if you prefer)
2 tablespoons chopped fresh chives

**MEATBALLS**

1 kg (2 lb 3 oz) minced (ground) chicken
½ cup finely grated parmesan cheese
⅓ cup packaged dried breadcrumbs
1 egg
1 teaspoon cracked black pepper
½ teaspoon garlic powder
½ teaspoon onion powder
½ teaspoon dried rosemary
½ teaspoon dried thyme

1. Combine all the meatball ingredients in a large mixing bowl. Use clean hands (or wear disposable gloves) to mix together, then roll into about 40 small meatballs.

2. Place half the Buffalo wing sauce into the slow cooker. Gently place the meatballs into the sauce. A single layer is ideal but if you have to double up some that's okay too.

3. Pour the remaining Buffalo wing sauce over the meatballs.

4. Cover and cook on low for 3½ hours. Do NOT stir the meatballs or move them until the final hour. This will ensure they stay intact perfectly. They can be gently stirred in that last hour to ensure they are well coated in the sauce.

5. To serve, place meatballs on a serving plate with some of the buffalo sauce spooned over. Drizzle meatballs lightly with aioli (or ranch dressing). Scatter with chives. If serving as finger food, place a toothpick into each meatball.

# Saucy and Sweet Pork Steaks

While this recipe uses pork scotch fillet steaks, you could also use pork chops or pork fillet. They would all go well with this Asian inspired sauce!

**Preparation** 10 mins • **Cook** 5 hours • **Cooker capacity** 6 litres • **Serves** 4

1 kg (2 lb 3 oz) pork scotch fillet steaks
¼ cup sweet chilli sauce
¼ cup salt-reduced soy sauce
1 tablespoon minced garlic
2 teaspoons minced ginger
½ cup honey
½ cup tomato sauce (ketchup)
1 tablespoon white vinegar
1 tablespoon cornflour (cornstarch), optional

1. Place the steaks into the slow cooker.

2. Combine the other ingredients (except cornflour) and pour over.

3. Cover and cook on low for 5 hours.

4. To thicken the sauce, mix the cornflour with 2 tablespoons water and stir into the sauce for the last 15 mins of cooking. Alternatively, remove the steaks from the slow cooker, cover and set aside. Pour the sauce into a small saucepan and cook over high heat for 5–10 minutes, to reduce and thicken.

# Spaghetti Bolognaise

I constantly have folks tell me that my spaghetti sauce is the best they've ever tasted, and after trying this recipe they never cook it any other way! The ingredients are just something that evolved over the many years I've been cooking it, which is nearly every week because it's a firm favourite in our house. Kids LOVE spaghetti night and it's always a go-to for me on nights I have extra mouths to feed, as a little goes a long way. This recipe freezes well and can also be multiplied to make a bigger batch.

**Preparation** 15 mins • **Cook** 5 hours • **Cooker capacity** 5 litres • **Serves** 6

500 g (1 lb 2 oz) minced (ground) lean beef
500 g (1 lb 2 oz) jar tomato-based pasta sauce
200 g condensed tomato soup (half 420 g/15 oz can)
2–3 garlic cloves, finely chopped
1 brown onion, finely diced
8 mushrooms, roughly chopped
1 large carrot, grated
1 teaspoon dried Italian herbs
¼ cup BBQ sauce
2 tablespoons Worcestershire sauce
Cooked spaghetti
Grated cheese (parmesan or tasty), to serve

1. Combine all the ingredients (except the spaghetti and cheese) in the slow cooker (no need to brown the mince first).

2. Cover and cook on low for 5 hours (this recipe copes well with the 'keep warm' setting after the cooking time is complete). Meanwhile, cook the spaghetti to packet instructions.

3. Place the drained pasta into serving bowls and spoon over the Bolognaise sauce.

4. Serve topped with grated cheese.

# Chicken and Leek Pie

Who doesn't love a beautiful home-cooked pie – especially when the flavours of chicken and leek go together so well! We like to serve this with sweet potato mash and peas, or other steamed green vegetables of your choice. While we like to make this filling into a large family pie, it could be used to make individual pies in a pie maker. It can also be served without any pastry topping as a chicken and leek casserole.

**Preparation** 20 mins • **Cook** 6 hours 20 mins • **Cooker capacity** 5 litres • **Serves** 6

1 kg (2 lb 3 oz) skinless chicken thigh fillets, chopped
2 tablespoons cornflour (cornstarch)
1 leek, white and pale green part only
2 small carrots, finely diced
1 tablespoon wholegrain mustard
420 g (15 oz) can condensed cream of chicken soup
1 teaspoon dried thyme
1–2 sheets frozen puff pastry
1 egg yolk, lightly beaten

1. Place chicken in a large plastic bag with the cornflour and shake to coat. Add the floured chicken to the slow cooker.

2. Cut the leek lengthways into quarters then thinly slice. Add to slow cooker, along with the carrots, mustard, soup and thyme. Season with salt and pepper and give everything a good stir to combine.

3. Cover and cook on low for 6 hours.

4. Preheat the oven to 220°C (425°F). Lightly spray a large (about 2 litre [4 pint] capacity) pie dish or ovenproof dish with spray oil. Add the chicken mixture.

5. Cover top of pie dish with pastry, trimming and joining to fit as needed. Brush with beaten egg yolk. Make 2 small slits in the pastry centre to allow steam to escape.

6. Bake for 15–20 minutes or until golden brown.

# Shredded Beef Ragu

This flavour-packed, meaty pasta sauce is an 'add it all to the pot and walk away' kind of recipe, which I love! After cooking you come back and shred the meat, then toss through some pappardelle pasta and serve everything sprinkled with parmesan. If you are feeling it, add some garlic bread so everyone can mop up all the delicious last little bits.

**Preparation** 15 mins • **Cook** 6 hours • **Cooker capacity** 6 litres • **Serves** 6

800 g–1 kg (1 lb 12 oz–2 lb 3 oz) beef roast (blade or topside)
1 brown onion, finely diced
2 carrots, finely diced
2 celery stalks, finely diced
4 garlic cloves, minced
2 beef stock cubes, crumbled (or 2 teaspoons beef stock powder)
1 teaspoon dried thyme
1 teaspoon dried oregano
700 g (1 lb 9 oz) bottle passata (pureed tomato)
400 g (14 oz) can diced tomatoes
2 tablespoons tomato paste (concentrated puree)
¼ cup red wine (I use cabernet merlot)
2 teaspoons sugar
2 sprigs fresh rosemary (or 1 teaspoon dried)
2 bay leaves
Pappardelle (the really wide ribbons), to serve
Chopped parsley and finely grated parmesan, to serve

1. Place all the ingredients (except the pasta, parsley and parmesan) into the slow cooker.

2. Cover and cook on high for 6 hours.

3. Remove the bay leaves and rosemary sprigs and discard.

4. Gently lift the meat out. Use 2 forks to shred the meat, then return it to the slow cooker and stir through the sauce.

5. Turn the slow cooker down to low and leave it so the meat can soak up the sauce while you cook the pasta according to the packet instructions.

6. Place the drained pasta into a large serving bowl and gently toss through the meat sauce to coat.

7. Serve topped with parsley and parmesan.

# Roast Lamb Obsession

This remains one of the most popular recipes I've ever created. Originally intended for lamb chops, it then became popular with lamb shanks and also roast lamb. It makes the most mouth-watering gravy to serve with the meat and any veggies you like. Leftovers are great the next day in lamb and gravy rolls. It's also suitable to freeze. A firm favourite all over the world!

**Preparation** 10 mins • **Cook** 8 hours • **Cooker capacity** 6 litres • **Serves** 6

1.5 kg (3 lb 5 oz) boneless lamb leg or shoulder roast
1 brown onion, chopped
420 g (15 oz) can condensed cream of mushroom soup
40 g (1½ oz) packet French onion soup mix
2 tablespoons Worcestershire sauce
2 tablespoons mint sauce

1. Place the lamb and onion into the slow cooker.

2. Combine all the other ingredients and pour over.

3. Cover and cook on low for 8 hours.

4. To serve, slice the meat thickly, or shred if you prefer.

# Notes

# Set 5 Shopping List

**MEAT**
2 kg (4 lb 6 oz) chicken drumsticks
1 kg (2 lb 3 oz) chicken mince
1 kg (2 lb 3 oz) pork scotch fillet steaks
500 g (1 lb 2 oz) lean mince beef
1 kg (2 lb 3 oz) chicken thigh fillets
800 g–1 kg (1 lb 12 oz–2 lb 3 oz) beef roast
(blade or topside)
1.5 g (3 lb 5 oz) lamb roast

**COLD PRODUCTS**
500 g (1 lb 2 oz) bag diced frozen vegetables
1 cup grated parmesan cheese
2 eggs
1 cup grated cheddar cheese
2 sheets frozen puff pastry

**FRESH PRODUCE**
5 onions
2 tablespoons fresh chives
7 cloves fresh garlic
8 mushrooms
5 carrots
1 leek
2 stalks celery
2 sprigs fresh rosemary (or extra 1 teaspoon
dried)

**PANTRY**
40 g (1½ oz) sachet dry chicken noodle soup
mix
¼ cup good quality chicken stock powder (or
6 cubes)
2 teaspoons beef stock powder (or 2 cubes)
⅓ cup fine dried packaged breadcrumbs
400 g (14 oz) bottle Buffalo wing sauce
1 x 500 g (1 lb 2 oz) jar tomato based pasta/
spaghetti sauce

700 g (1 lb 9 oz) bottle tomato passata
400 g (14 oz) can of diced/crushed tomato
2 tablespoons concentrated tomato paste
1 x 200 g (7 oz) can of tomato soup
1 x 420 g (13 oz) can condensed cream of
chicken soup
1 x 420 g (13 oz) can condensed cream of
mushroom soup
1 x 40 g (1½ oz) sachet dry French onion
soup mix
500 g (1 lb 2 oz) spaghetti
500 g (1 lb 2 oz) pappardelle
½ teaspoons garlic powder
½ teaspoons onion powder
½ teaspoons dried rosemary
2½ teaspoons dried thyme
1 teaspoons dried Italian herbs
1 teaspoons dried oregano
4 tablespoons aioli dressing (or ranch
dressing)
¼ cup sweet chilli sauce
¼ cup soy sauce (I prefer salt reduced)
1 tablespoon wholegrain mustard
½ cup red wine
1 tablespoon minced garlic
2 teaspoons minced ginger
½ cup honey
½ cup tomato sauce
¼ cup BBQ sauce
3 tablespoons Worcestershire sauce
2 tablespoons mint sauce (or some fresh
mint leaves if you prefer)
1 tablespoon vinegar
2 bay leave
2 teaspoons sugar
Cornflour
Cracked black pepper
Salt

# Extras

_____

_____

_____

_____

_____

_____

_____

_____

_____

_____

_____

_____

_____

_____

_____

_____

_____

_____

# Set 6

Tomato and Bacon Soup

Pasta Bake

Steak in Creamy Mushroom Sauce

Lamb Surprise

Oyster Asian Chicken

Whole Chicken Korma

Marinated Roast Beef

# Tomato and Bacon Soup

There is something just so right about the pairing of tomato and bacon! With the addition of fresh basil and vegetables this soup is both nutritious and delicious. Served with a generous dollop of mascarpone it not only looks amazing but it tastes incredible too! You'll find mascarpone in a tub in the cheese fridge at the supermarket. Once you have tried it, you'll want to use it on EVERYTHING, it is so yummy. Leftover soup is great to freeze for extra-easy meals on busy days. If you want to impress, this soup is amazing served in a hollowed out crusty sourdough bread roll as a bowl.

Preparation 20 mins • Cook 6 hours • Cooker capacity 6 litres • Serves 6

SOUP
2 x 800 g (1 lb 12 oz) cans diced tomatoes
2 small brown onions, diced
2 celery stalks, sliced
1 large carrot, finely diced
1 tablespoon minced garlic
1 cup vegetable stock
300 g (10½ oz) diced bacon
½ teaspoon salt
½ teaspoon cracked black pepper
Handful fresh basil leaves, sliced
1 teaspoon dried thyme
2 teaspoons smoked paprika
2 tablespoons Worcestershire sauce
150 ml (5½ fl oz) cooking cream

TOPPING
1 large dollop mascarpone per person, to serve
Chopped fresh chives, to garnish

1. Combine the soup ingredients (except the cream) in the slow cooker.

2. Cover and cook on low for 6 hours.

3. Using a stick blender, blend the soup to a smooth consistency. Stir through the cooking cream.

4. Serve topped with a generous dollop of mascarpone and a scattering of chives.

# Pasta Bake

This cheesy mince and pasta bake is always a hit with the kids! We simply serve and enjoy as is (great on a cold night as a warm belly filler), but you could serve some steamed vegetables too if you like. Leftovers reheat well in the microwave, so you can take some to work the next day and that's two meals taken care of!

**Preparation** 15 mins • **Cook** 3 hours 15 mins • **Cooker capacity** 5 litres • **Serves** 6

1 kg (2 lb 3 oz) minced (ground) lean beef
1 large brown onion, diced
400 g (14 oz) can condensed cream of mushroom soup
¼ cup BBQ sauce
2 tablespoons Worcestershire sauce
2 beef stock cubes, crumbled
1 teaspoon dried Italian herbs
2 garlic cloves, minced
2 cups penne
2 cups grated tasty or cheddar cheese
2 tablespoons chopped fresh chives

1. Combine the mince, onion, soup, sauces, stock cubes, herbs and garlic in the slow cooker and mix well.

2. Cover and cook on high for 2½ hours. Stir occasionally during cooking if you are nearby, or if not, give it a good stir at the end to break up any lumps.

3. Bring a large saucepan of water to the boil towards the end of the cooking time.

4. Add the penne and boil for just 5 minutes. It should be starting to become tender before you add it to the slow cooker, and par-boiling first ensures it doesn't absorb all the liquid in the slow cooker (it will still soak up a little). Drain pasta well then add to the slow cooker and gently mix to combine.

5. Cover and cook for a further 30 minutes.

6. Sprinkle with the grated cheese then the chives.

7. Cook, covered, for about 15 minutes more to melt the cheese. This final step can be done in a hot oven for a few minutes if you wish it to brown. Some slow cooker bowls are ovenproof, but if in doubt, transfer the mixture to an oven-safe dish to do this. This oven step is completely optional. Your pasta bake will still taste delicious served straight from the slow cooker.

# Steak in Creamy Mushroom Sauce

If you are someone who chooses a mushroom sauce when you order steak then you'll love this recipe! The steak is absolutely 'melt in your mouth' tender. You'll definitely want a slice of buttered bread on hand to wipe up every last bit of the gravy at the end of your meal – you can thank me later.

**Preparation** 10 mins • **Cook** 5 hours • **Cooker capacity** 5 litres • **Serves** 4

1 kg (2 lb 3 oz) beef chuck or rump steaks
300 g (10½ oz) mushrooms, quartered
2 teaspoons beef stock powder
500 ml (17 fl oz) cooking cream
2 tablespoons cornflour (cornstarch)

1. Place the steaks into the slow cooker and top with the mushrooms.
2. Whisk the stock powder into the cooking cream then pour over the steaks and mushrooms.
3. Cover and cook on low for 4½ hours.
4. Carefully remove the steaks from the slow cooker (I use 2 egg flips to lift them out so they stay intact). Set aside.
5. Combine the cornflour with 2 tablespoons water and whisk into the mushroom sauce.
6. Gently return the steaks to the sauce. Cover, putting a tea towel (dish towel) under the lid. Increase to HIGH and cook for 30 minutes to thicken the sauce.
7. Gently lift the steaks out onto a serving dish and top with the creamy mushroom sauce.

#  Lamb Surprise

Many people are surprised by one of the ingredients in this dish ... the cola. But then they are even more surprised by how delicious and tender it makes this lamb taste! Go ahead ... trust the process – you'll be pleasantly surprised too. This is an absolutely finger-licking delicious dish that the whole family devours! Serve the lamb shredded in the gravy with mashed potatoes and steamed veggies. Leftovers make a great saucy lamb roll for lunch the next day!

**Preparation** 10 mins • **Cook** 9 hours 15 mins • **Cooker capacity** 6 litres • **Serves** 6

1.5 kg (3 lb 5 oz) lamb leg roast
375 ml (12½ fl oz) can cola
40 g (1½ oz) packet French onion soup mix
1 cup sweet chilli sauce
1 tablespoon cornflour (cornstarch)

1. Place the lamb into the slow cooker.
2. Combine the cola, soup mix and sauce and pour over the lamb.
3. Cover and cook on low for 9 hours.
4. Remove the lamb from the slow cooker. Discard any bone, shred the meat and return it to the slow cooker.
5. Combine the cornflour with 2 tablespoons water and stir into the lamb mixture. Cover and cook for a further 10–15 minutes to thicken, then serve with lots of the delicious sauce.

#  Oyster Asian Chicken

These tasty chicken drumsticks are great served with fried rice and salad. You could even marinate them in the sauce the night before for extra flavour if you'd prefer. It would work well with wings too!

**Preparation** 10 mins • **Cook** 4 hours • **Cooker capacity** 6 litres • **Serves** 5

10 chicken drumsticks
1 tablespoon minced garlic
½ cup oyster sauce
¼ cup teriyaki sauce
¼ cup honey
2 tablespoons soy sauce
2 tablespoons tomato sauce (ketchup)
1 tablespoon brown sugar

1. Place the chicken into the slow cooker.

2. Combine all the other ingredients and pour over the chicken.

3. Cover and cook on low for 4 hours, turning and basting with sauce occasionally during cooking for a rich colour.

# ◼— Whole Chicken Korma —●

This is something different to do with your next whole chicken! It's full of flavour and super juicy. Cut it into quarters to serve, or debone and shred it into the sauce. Serve either option on rice. Turn to pages 18–19 for tips on cooking a whole chicken.

**Preparation** 15 mins • **Cook** 6 hours • **Cooker capacity** 6 litres • **Serves** 4

1 whole chicken
1 red onion, thinly sliced
1 red capsicum (pepper), thinly sliced
270 ml (9½ fl oz) can coconut cream
¼ cup korma curry paste
1 tablespoon minced ginger
2 garlic cloves, minced
1 tablespoon brown sugar
2 teaspoons fish sauce
1 lime, zest finely grated, juiced
½ bunch fresh coriander, chopped
Extra coriander and lime wedges, to serve

1. Spray the slow cooker bowl lightly with oil spray.

2. Place the chicken into the slow cooker, breast side down. Top with the onion and half the capsicum slices.

3. Combine the coconut cream, curry paste, ginger, garlic, sugar, fish sauce, lime zest, juice and coriander. Stir well then pour over the chicken.

4. Cover and cook on low for 5 hours, but add an extra hour if the chicken is over 2 kg (4 lb 6 oz).

5. After 4hrs of cooking, add the remaining capsicum slices (keeping a few slices for a final garnish). Adding the remaining capsicum in the last hour rather than all at the beginning gives extra colour to the final dish.

6. Carefully lift the chicken from the slow cooker. You can either portion it into quarters, or pull the meat from the bones and shred it.

7. Divide the chicken between serving plates and pour the sauce over. Finely dice the reserved capsicum. Finely dice the reserved capsicum slices and scatter over the top, along with some extra coriander. Serve with a lime wedge on the side, with steamed rice.

# Marinated Roast Beef

Tender, slow cooked roast beef is everything you could want at the end of a long week! Serve it with traditional roast vegetables and your favourite gravy. You could also slice it and serve it in bread rolls with gravy for a great entertaining option straight from your slow cooker. Alternatively, thinly slice it and have it for a work day sandwich filling!

**Preparation** 10 mins + marinating • **Cook** 6½ hours • **Cooker capacity** 5 litres • **Serves** 6

> 1.5 kg (3 lb 5 oz) beef roast (I used a porterhouse roast but a cheaper cut will
>   work fine)
> 1 tablespoon minced garlic
> ⅓ cup salt-reduced soy sauce
> ¼ cup olive oil
> 2 tablespoons white vinegar
> 2 tablespoons maple syrup
> 2 tablespoons Dijon mustard
> 1 tablespoon Worcestershire sauce
> 2 teaspoons onion powder
> 2 teaspoons dried thyme
> 2 teaspoons cracked black pepper
> 1 teaspoon dried rosemary

1. Place the beef into a large zip-lock bag.

2. Combine all the other ingredients and pour into the bag with the meat. Seal tightly.

3. Place the bag into the fridge to marinate for a minimum of 4 hours, or up to 36 hours. I prepare it one morning then cook it the following night.

4. Remove the meat from the bag and place into the slow cooker. Discard the remaining marinade.

5. Cover and cook on low for 6½ hours. Turn off the slow cooker and allow the meat to rest for 15 minutes to reabsorb liquids and become juicy and delicious.

**Note:** We serve this with seasoned roast potatoes, steamed broccolini, carrots, peas, green beans and a drizzle of gravy. When making gravy, replace some of the required water with cooking juices from the slow cooker for extra flavour.

# Notes

# Set 6 Shopping List

**MEAT**
300 g (10½ oz) diced bacon
1 kg (2 lb 3 oz) lean beef mince
1 kg (2 lb 3 oz) beef chuck steaks (or rump
    steaks)
1.5 kg (3 lb 5 oz) lamb roast
1.5 kg (3 lb 5 oz) beef roast
10 chicken drumsticks
1 whole chicken

**COLD PRODUCTS**
650 ml (22 fl oz) cooking cream
1 tub mascarpone cheese
2 cups grated tasty or cheddar cheese

**FRESH PRODUCE**
3 onions
1 red onion
1 red capsicum
2 celery stalks
1 carrot
300 g (10½ oz) mushrooms
15–20 g (½–¾ oz) fresh basil leaves
4 tablespoons fresh chives
2 limes
½ bunch fresh coriander

**PANTRY**
2 x 800 g (1 lb 12 oz) cans diced/crushed
    tomatoes
1 x 400 g (14 oz) can condensed cream of
    mushroom soup
270 ml (9 fl oz) coconut cream

¼ cup korma paste
375 ml (12½ fl oz) can of cola
1 x 40 g (1½ oz) sachet of dry French onion
    soup
1 cup sweet chilli sauce
2 tablespoons maple syrup
2 tablespoons Dijon mustard
5 tablespoons Worcestershire sauce
¼ cup BBQ sauce
½ cup oyster sauce
¼ cup teriyaki sauce
2 teaspoons fish sauce
2 tablespoons tomato sauce
¼ cup honey
125 ml (4¼ fl oz) soy sauce (I prefer reduced
    salt)
¼ cup olive oil
4 teaspoons beef stock powder (or 4 cubes)
2 cups penne
5 tablespoons minced garlic
1 tablespoon minced ginger
2 tablespoons white vinegar
1 cup liquid vegetable stock
3 teaspoons dried thyme
2 teaspoons onion powder
1 teaspoons dried rosemary
2 teaspoons smoked paprika
1 teaspoons dried Italian herbs
2 tablespoons brown sugar
Cornflour
Cracked black pepper
Salt

# Extras

# Set 7

Pumpkin and Sweet Potato Soup

Rissoles in Rich Gravy

Sweet Lamb Curry

Whole Chicken with Garlic Butter and Soy

Asian Beef Udon Noodles

Beef Stroganoff

Rolled Turkey Roast and Vegetables

# Pumpkin and Sweet Potato Soup

A thick, vegetarian soup packed full of pure nutritious goodness. Leftovers freeze well so this is one I make often and portion up in serves to freeze for work lunches or dinners on the run. It reheats well in a microwave in minutes. Note that the first step of oven roasting the vegetables is optional and can be bypassed to save time on busy days – it still tastes amazing either way!

**Preparation** 20 mins • **Cook** 6½ or 8½ hours • **Cooker capacity** 6 litres • **Serves** 8

1 butternut pumpkin, cut into large dice
1 large sweet potato, cut into large dice
3 medium potatoes, cut into dice
2 brown onions, chopped
2 large carrots, sliced
2 teaspoons minced garlic
4–8 cups (1–2 L) vegetable stock (see note)

1. Preheat the oven to 180°C (160°C fan-forced). Arrange the pumpkin and sweet potato on a large baking tray lined with baking paper and roast for 30 minutes, until partially cooked. Place into the slow cooker.

2. Add the remaining ingredients to the slow cooker.

3. Cover and cook on high for 3 hours then low for 3 hours. Alternatively, you can cook on low for 8 hours.

4. Using a stick blender, blend the soup to a smooth consistency. Alternatively, take out half the soup, blend the remaining soup then return the first amount back to the slow cooker. This leaves a bit of texture in the soup.

**Notes:** Roasting the pumpkin and sweet potato gives a delicious depth of flavour to the soup, but you could skip it and just add all the ingredients raw, to save on prep time. I use 4 cups of stock for a really thick soup, or 8 cups for a runnier soup.

# Rissoles in Rich Gravy

This recipe was deliberately made using purchased rissoles, especially for time-poor families who need something to get cooking in next to no time on a hectic day – we all have those days! You can pick up a tray of raw rissoles from your butcher or supermarket meat department, but by all means if you prefer to roll your own rissoles you can (there is a great rissole recipe from scratch on page 192).

Preparation 10 mins • Cook 5–6 hours • Cooker capacity 6 litres • Serves 6

1 large brown onion, sliced
500 ml (17 fl oz) gravy (made from powder – see note)
12 beef rissoles
1 teaspoon dried rosemary
1 teaspoon dried oregano
Mashed potato and steamed green beans, to serve

1. Place the onion slices over the base of the slow cooker.

2. Pour the gravy over the onions. Sit the rissoles on top and sprinkle with the herbs.

3. Cover and cook on low for 5–6 hours – you can gently turn them over halfway through cooking, if you are around to do so.

4. If you wish to thicken gravy, gently remove the rissoles and set aside, covered, to keep warm. Reduce the gravy using the slow cooker searing mode or transfer to a saucepan and cook on the stovetop briefly over high heat, stirring constantly.

5. Serve with creamy mashed potato and steamed greens.

**Notes:** I use gravy powder which calls for 50 g (1 ¾ oz) powder to 500 ml (17 fl oz) water. If you are using a regular sachet-style gravy it usually makes 250 ml (9 fl oz) of gravy, so you'll need 2 sachets. Be sure to make the gravy with cold tap water, as it will heat during the slow cooking.

# Sweet Lamb Curry

When I first created this recipe, I had yet to find a curry I enjoyed. I had begun to think curries just weren't my thing. Then one night when I was working the evening shift in the psychiatric ward I nurse in, I was handing out the dinner trays when … I smelled something. It smelled so yummy I had to find a menu card to read what it was … 'lamb curry'. Later that week after reading everything I could about lamb curries I perfected this recipe. To this day, even though I now love curries of all sorts, this is still my favourite curry ever!

**Preparation 15 mins • Cook 8 hours • Cooker capacity 5 litres • Serves 6**

1 kg (2 lb 3 oz) diced lamb
1 large brown onion, diced
2 garlic cloves, minced
3 teaspoons mild curry powder
½ teaspoon minced ginger
2 small Granny Smith apples, peeled, cored and diced
½ cup beef stock
½ cup fruit chutney
2 tablespoons cornflour (cornstarch)
Mashed potato or rice and crusty bread rolls, to serve

1. Place all the ingredients (except the cornflour) into the slow cooker.

2. Cover and cook on low for 7½ hours.

3. Mix the cornflour with 1 tablespoon water, then stir through the lamb mixture.

4. Cover and cook for a further 30 minutes, to thicken the sauce.

5. Serve with creamy mashed potato or rice and crusty bread rolls.

**Note:** You could ask your butcher to debone and dice a leg of lamb if you like.

# Whole Chicken with Garlic Butter and Soy

We cook this chicken and then shred all the meat from the bones to serve on wraps with lettuce and cheese for an easy light dinner. It's also great to shred and have on hand for lunchbox salads and sandwiches. Of course, you could also serve it hot with vegetables as a roast dinner if you prefer. So versatile! So yummy! Turn to pages 18–19 for tips on cooking a whole chicken.

**Preparation** 15 mins • **Cook** 6 hours • **Cooker capacity** 6 litres • **Serves** 4–6

1 whole chicken, about 2 kg (4 lb 6 oz)
75 g (2½ oz) butter, softened
1 tablespoon minced garlic
⅓ cup kecap manis (see note)

1. Place the chicken on a cutting board and loosen the skin on the breast. It will lift fairly easily away from the flesh, and you can work your fingers into it to form a pocket.

2. Combine the butter and garlic. Spoon the garlic butter into the pocket under the skin. Taking care not to break the skin, work it down towards the tail of the chicken and all over the breast meat under the skin. Gently reshape the skin neatly over the breast.

3. Place the chicken breast side down into the slow cooker

4. Brush kecap manis over the chicken.

5. Cover and cook on low for 6 hours, brushing regularly with the cooking liquids to create a rich golden brown colour on the finished chicken.

6. Remove the meat from the bones and shred, or carve the chicken into pieces.

**Note:** Kecap manis is an Indonesian soy sauce, and it is much sweeter and more thick and syrupy than regular soy sauce.

# Asian Beef Udon Noodles

Save yourself the expense of take-away noodles and enjoy a much healthier alternative from home. These beef and vegetable noodles are popular with the whole family for a fraction of the cost!

**Preparation** 20 mins • **Cook** 4 hours • **Cooker capacity** 6 litres • **Serves** 4

700 g (1 lb 9 oz) minced (ground) beef
1 large brown onion, cut into thin strips
1 large carrot, cut into very thin sticks
1 bunch baby pak choy, each piece halved lengthways then crossways
½ cup oyster sauce
½ cup soy sauce
¼ cup mirin
2 tablespoons brown sugar
1 tablespoon rice wine vinegar
440 g (15½ oz) packet wok-ready udon noodles
4 green onions/scallions/eschallots, thinly sliced

1. Place all the ingredients (except the noodles and green onions) into the slow cooker and mix well.

2. Cover and cook on low for 4 hours, mixing once or twice to break up any lumps of mince.

3. Prepare the noodles as per package instructions (usually this is just soak in boiling water for 2–3 minutes). Drain well.

4. Add the noodles and green onions to the slow cooker and toss to coat and mix through. Serve immediately.

**Note:** Mirin is available from the Asian section at the supermarket.

#  Beef Stroganoff

This is a lush, decadent, creamy beef stroganoff with a dash of brandy for extra 'ooh la la'! The addition of brandy and thick 'dollop' cream was a great tip given to me by my friend Sarah who said her sister Rachel makes THE BEST strog with these additions, and she wasn't wrong! It goes perfectly with creamy mashed potato, chopped parsley and your favourite steamed veggies. Some people prefer their stroganoff served with pasta, so you may like that option.

Preparation 20 mins • Cook 6 hours • Cooker capacity 3.5 litres • Serves 5

1 kg (2 lb 3 oz) beef strips
2 tablespoons cornflour (cornstarch)
2 tablespoons butter
1 large brown onion, sliced
250 g (9 oz) button mushrooms, sliced
⅔ cup beef stock
50 ml (1¾ fl oz) brandy
2 tablespoons tomato paste (concentrated puree)
1 tablespoon Worcestershire sauce
2 teaspoons mustard
1½ teaspoons smoked paprika
200 ml (6 ¾ fl oz) thick cream ('dollop' type)
2 teaspoons cornflour (cornstarch), extra
Chopped fresh parsley, to serve

1. Place the beef strips and cornflour into a large plastic bag and season with salt and pepper. Seal tightly and shake to coat.

2. Melt 2 teaspoons butter in a searing slow cooker or frying pan. Add the onion and cook over high heat for 2–3 minutes, until softened. Transfer to the slow cooker (if using frying pan) or set aside on a plate.

3. Melt another 2 teaspoons of butter in the cooker or frying pan and cook ⅓ of the beef just until browned. Repeat in 2 more batches.

4. Place the onions and browned beef in the slow cooker and add the mushrooms.

5. Combine the beef stock, brandy, tomato paste, sauce, mustard and paprika. Pour over the beef and onion and gently stir to combine.

6. Cover and cook on low for 5 hours 40 minutes.

7. Mix the cream and extra cornflour until smooth, then stir into the stroganoff. Cover and cook for a further 20 minutes, to thicken.

8. Scatter with parsley to serve.

# Rolled Turkey Roast and Vegetables

You'll love the simplicity of a moist rolled turkey roast and all your vegetables cooked at once in this one pot roast dinner winner! Turkey leftovers are great for lunch the next day too.

**Preparation** 20 mins • **Cook** 8 hours • **Cooker capacity** 6 litres • **Serves** 4–6

2 kg (4 lb 6 oz) turkey breast roast (see notes)
3 potatoes, cut into quarters
½ butternut pumpkin, cut into quarters
2 large carrots, left whole
1 large brown onion, left whole
1 large sweet potato, cut into quarters
4 large sprigs fresh rosemary
29 g (1 oz) instant gravy powder sachet

1. Line the slow cooker with baking paper and place the turkey in the centre.
2. Layer the vegetable pieces around the turkey, with the potatoes on the bottom then the sweet potato, pumpkin, carrots and onion.
3. Season with salt and pepper and lay the rosemary sprigs on top
4. Cover and cook on low for 8 hours.
5. Transfer the turkey to a cutting board and cover loosely with foil. Place the vegetables into a covered dish to keep warm while you make the gravy.
6. Make the gravy according to packet directions, using some liquid from the slow cooker to make up the water requirement for the gravy.
7. To serve, slice the turkey and cut the carrots and onion into serving pieces. Serve drizzled with gravy.

**Notes:** There's no need to add any liquid to the turkey; it will make plenty of its own while cooking.

I use a frozen rolled turkey roast, but it must be FULLY thawed before cooking. You could use a chicken rolled roast instead, if you prefer it to turkey.

# Notes

# Set 7 Shopping List

## MEATS
12 raw beef rissoles (thick meat patties)
1 kg (2 lb 3 oz) diced lamb
1 whole chicken
700 g (1 lb 9 oz) minced (ground) beef
1 kg (2 lb 3 oz) beef strips
2 kg (4 lb 6 oz) rolled turkey breast roast (or chicken)

## COLD PRODUCTS
125 g (4½ oz) butter
200 ml (7 fl oz) thick cream, 'dollop' style

## FRESH PRODUCE
1½ butternut pumpkins
2 sweet potatoes
6 potatoes
5 carrots
7 onions
250 g (9 oz) button mushrooms
2 Granny Smith apples or other green apples
1 bunch baby pak choy
4 green onions/scallions/eschalots
4 large sprigs fresh rosemary
¼ bunch fresh parsley

## PANTRY
3 tablespoons minced garlic
½ teaspoon minced ginger
1–2 litres (34–68 fl oz) liquid vegetable stock
1.5 cups liquid beef stock
½ cup fruit chutney
⅓ cup kecap manis (sweet soy sauce)
3 sachets instant gravy powder (2 traditional roast gravy, 1 chicken gravy)
1 teaspoons dried rosemary
1 teaspoon dried oregano
½ teaspoons smoked paprika
3 teaspoons mild curry powder
¼ cup mirin (available from supermarkets in the Asian section)
½ cup oyster sauce
½ cup soy sauce (I prefer reduced salt)
2 tablespoons brown sugar
1 tablespoon rice wine vinegar
440 g (1½ oz) packet wok-ready udon noodles
2 tablespoons tomato paste (concentrated puree)
2 teaspoons mustard
1 tablespoon Worcestershire sauce
50 ml (1¾ fl oz) brandy
Cornflour
Cracked black pepper
Salt

# Extras

# Set 8

Classic Pea and Ham Soup

Pickled Pork

Tuscan Meatballs

Steak Diane

Sticky French Chicken

Thai Red Curry Pork Fillet

Roast Lamb with Rosemary Butter and Red Wine

# Classic Pea and Ham Soup

Pea and ham soup is a classic slow cooker meal, but I like to make mine even easier by using ham that's already cut from the hock as sold by the butcher. Of course you could use 2–3 ham hocks, or even leftover Christmas ham. Once cooked, chop the meat, discard the bone with skin and fat, then return the meat to the soup. Leftovers freeze well for easy meals later on.

Preparation 10 mins • Cook 8 hours • Cooker capacity 6 litres • Serves 8

1–2 x 500 g (1 lb 2 oz) packets green split peas (see note), rinsed and drained
2 brown onions, diced
750 g (1 lb 11 oz) diced hock ham (or options discussed in recipe introduction)
Crusty bread stick slices, buttered, to serve

1. Place the split peas, onion and ham into the slow cooker and fill with water to a maximum of 2 inches below the top of the inner cooking bowl.

2. Cover and cook on low for 8 hours. If your slow cooker tends to cook on the slower side, I suggest increasing this time to 10 hours or doing half the time on high and half on low. It needs long or hot enough cooking to break down the split peas. This thickens the soup and gives it a lovely smooth consistency. The soup is very tolerant of cooking almost all on high so don't fear that you might overcook or burn it.

**Notes:** If you like a really thick, stick-to-your-sides kind of pea soup use two packets of split peas. If you prefer a thinner soup then one is enough.

#  Pickled Pork

I'd never cooked pickled pork before experimenting with this recipe, but it made an impression on my family and they asked to have it more often! It gave us all hot Christmas ham vibes! This is one of those recipes you can pop on in the morning and leave alone all day long with nothing more to do, so it's great for work days or just busy days. We serve ours with a creamy potato mash, steamed broccolini, sliced carrots and baby peas. You could serve a white, cheese or mustard sauce, but we loved it with our favourite gravy.

**Preparation** 10 mins • **Cook** 8–9 or 5–6 hours • **Cooker capacity** 3.5 litres • **Serves** 4

1.5 kg (3 lb 5 oz) pickled pork
⅓ cup brown sugar
¼ cup apple cider vinegar
20 whole black peppercorns
2 whole cloves
1 large brown onion, cut into quarters

1. Rinse the pork and place into the slow cooker.

2. Top the slow cooker up with water to just cover the pork. Add all the other ingredients.

3. Cover and cook on low for 8–9 hours (or 5–6 hours on high instead if you are short on time).

4. Drain pork, and slice to serve.

#  Tuscan Meatballs

Do you love meatballs like we love meatballs? There's something about them that kids love, parents love and everyone loves. These can be made in advance (the day before) to make mealtime easier. These meatballs are delicious served with vegetables or pasta – whichever your family loves best. We like mashed potato, corn cobs and julienned carrots.

**Preparation** 30 mins • **Cook** 4 hours 15 mins • **Cooker capacity** 5 litres • **Serves** 5

**MEATBALLS**
800 g (1 lb 12 oz) minced (ground) pork
½ cup packaged dried breadcrumbs
½ cup finely grated parmesan
1 egg
½ teaspoon garlic powder
½ teaspoon onion powder
2 tablespoons milk

**SAUCE**
300 ml (10 fl oz) cooking cream
2 garlic cloves, minced
½ cup oil-free semi-dried tomatoes, sliced into thin strips (see notes)
1 teaspoon dried rosemary
¼ cup finely grated parmesan
60 g (2 oz) baby spinach leaves

1. Combine all the meatball ingredients and roll into about 30 medium meatballs. Place meatballs into slow cooker.

2. Combine all the sauce ingredients (except spinach) and pour over the meatballs.

3. Cover and cook on low for 4 hours. Do not stir at all until at least 2 hours into the cooking time. After this time the meatballs will be firm and can be gently moved around without any breakage.

4. Gently stir through the spinach and cook for an additional 15 minutes so it wilts in the sauce. Serve immediately.

**Note:** If your semi-dried tomatoes are the kind that do come in oil, soak away this oil first on paper towels.

#  Steak Diane

A creamy smooth Diane gravy smothering melt-in-your-mouth tender steaks – what's not to love! Ideally choose an inexpensive cut of steak such as oyster blade, chuck, casserole or one with a little fat marbling through. These will give a moister result than an extra lean, more expensive cut – a great way to save money too! We serve ours with creamy mashed potato, corn cobs and steamed baby asparagus because this recipe makes loads of delicious sauce!

**Preparation** 15 mins • **Cook** 6–7 hours **Cooker capacity** 6 litres • **Serves** 4–8

1 large brown onion, sliced into rings
2 tablespoons cornflour (cornstarch)
2 teaspoons beef stock powder
8 oyster blade steaks, 1.2 kg (2 lb 10 oz) total weight
200 g (7 oz) button mushrooms, thickly sliced
400 g (14 oz) passata (pureed tomato)
300 ml (10 fl oz) cooking cream
1 tablespoon Worcestershire sauce
1 tablespoon Dijon mustard
1 teaspoon minced garlic
Mashed potato and steamed vegetables, to serve
Fresh parsley, chopped, to garnish

1. Lay the onion slices over the bottom of the slow cooker bowl.

2. Place the cornflour, stock powder and steaks into a large plastic bag. Seal tightly and shake to coat.

3. Lay the coated steaks on top of the onions and top with the mushroom slices.

4. Combine the passata, cream, sauce, mustard and garlic and pour over the mushrooms.

5. Cover and cook on low for 6–7 hours, depending on your slow cooker (or until lovely and tender).

6. Serve steaks with lashings of the sauce on mash and steamed veg, with a sprinkling of parsley.

# Sticky French Chicken

This is one of those recipes that, when I first cooked it, I immediately wished I'd cooked twice as much. We were all scraping every little bit off our plates and looking for more. For me it was also really appealing that it was so simple to cook with just three ingredients! Serve it with rice or creamy mash and your favourite veggies. It works equally well with chicken drumsticks.

**Preparation** 10 mins • **Cook** 4 hours • **Cooker capacity** 5 litres • **Serves** 4

1 kg (2 lb 3 oz) skinless chicken thigh fillets
⅔ cup honey
40 g (1½ oz) packet French onion soup mix
1 tablespoon cornflour (cornstarch), optional

1. Add all the ingredients (except cornflour) to the slow cooker and mix to coat the chicken well.

2. Cover and cook on low for 4 hours.

3. If you would like to thicken the sauce, mix the cornflour with 2 tablespoons of water until smooth. Stir into the sauce, cover and cook for another 10 minutes.

# Thai Red Curry Pork Fillet

These thickly sliced pieces of pork fillet in red curry sauce are perfect served on rice. I would rate the spice level as mild to medium, but you can add more curry paste if you prefer it a little spicier.

**Preparation** 15 mins • **Cook** 4 hours • **Cooker capacity** 5 litres • **Serves** 4

2 pork fillets, about 400 g (14 oz) each
¾ cup sweet chilli sauce
½ cup smooth peanut butter
2 tablespoons red curry paste
2 tablespoons fresh lime juice
2 tablespoons fish sauce
2–3 tablespoons crushed peanuts, to serve
Fresh coriander, to serve
Steamed rice, to serve

1. Place the whole pork fillets into the slow cooker.

2. Combine the remaining ingredients (except those for serving) and pour over the pork.

3. Cover and cook on low for 4 hours. If you are around, turn the pork over halfway through cooking, coating evenly with the sauce mixture. It will still cook through if you can't turn it, but turning will give better colour on both sides.

4. Cut the pork into thick slices and serve on rice, with a scattering of crushed peanuts and coriander.

# Roast Lamb with Rosemary Butter and Red Wine

If you've never rubbed your roast with a garlic butter coating before cooking you've been missing out! This classic rosemary and garlic flavour combination complements your roast lamb and comes with a lush red wine sauce to pour over your finished dish.

**Preparation** 15 mins • **Cook** 5 or 8 hours • **Cooker capacity** 6 litres • **Serves** 6

1.5 kg boneless lamb leg or shoulder roast (3 lb 5 oz)
1½ tablespoons soft butter
1 teaspoon dried rosemary (or 2 teaspoons chopped fresh)
1 heaped teaspoon minced garlic
¼ teaspoon each salt and cracked black pepper
¾ cup hot water
½ cup red wine (Shiraz if you have it)
1 tablespoon vegetable stock powder
1 tablespoon tomato paste (concentrated puree)
1 tablespoon cornflour (cornstarch)

1. Place the lamb roast into the slow cooker.

2. Combine the butter, rosemary, garlic, salt and pepper and mix well.

3. Use the back of a spoon to spread the butter over the top and sides of the lamb.

4. Place the hot water, wine, stock powder and tomato paste in a jug and stir until well combined.

5. Pour into the slow cooker around the lamb, but not over the butter.

6. Cover and cook on high for 5 hours (or low for 8 hours). As the lamb cooks the butter will melt, and you can baste the meat with the buttery cooking juices occasionally if you are around.

7. Remove the lamb from the slow cooker and set aside to rest.

8. Skim and discard any excess fat from the liquid in the slow cooker. Combine the cornflour with 2 tablespoons water until smooth, then stir into the sauce. Transfer to a saucepan and cook over high heat on the stovetop until thickened to a gravy consistency.

9. Slice the lamb and serve with the red wine gravy poured over.

# Notes

# Set 8 Shopping List

## MEAT
750 g (1 lb 11 oz) diced hock ham
(or 2–3 whole hocks)
1.5 g (3 lb 5 oz) piece pickled pork
800 g (1 lb 12 oz) minced (ground) pork
8 medium oyster blade steaks (1.2 kg)
1 kg (2 lb 3 oz) skinless chicken thigh fillets
2 x 400–450 g (14 oz–1 lb) pork fillets
1.5 g (3 lb 5 oz) boneless lamb leg or
shoulder roast

## COLD PRODUCTS
¾ cup grated parmesan cheese
1 egg
2 tablespoons milk
600 ml (20 fl oz) cooking cream
1½ tablespoons salted butter

## FRESH PRODUCE
4 onions
1 lime
60 g (2 oz) baby spinach leaves
200 g (7 oz) button mushrooms
¼ bunch fresh coriander
¼ bunch fresh parsley

## PANTRY
1–2 x 500 g (1 lb 2 oz) packets dried green
split peas
¼ cup apple cider vinegar
5 teaspoons minced garlic (or 3 fresh cloves)
20 whole black peppercorns
2 whole dried cloves
400 g (14 oz) passata (pureed tomato)
1 tablespoon Worcestershire sauce
1 tablespoon Dijon mustard
⅓ cup brown sugar
2 teaspoons beef stock powder
½ cup packaged dried breadcrumbs
½ cup oil-free semi-dried
(add two hyphens) tomatoes
2 teaspoons dried rosemary
½ teaspoons garlic powder
½ teaspoons onion powder
⅔ cup honey
1 x 40 g (1½ oz) sachet dry French onion
soup mix
2 tablespoons red curry paste
2 tablespoons fish sauce
¾ cup sweet chilli sauce
½ cup smooth peanut butter
2–3 tablespoons crushed peanuts
½ cup red wine eg Shiraz
1 tablespoon vegetable stock powder
(or 2 cubes)
1 tablespoon tomato paste (concentrated
puree)
Cornflour
Cracked black pepper
Salt

# Extras

# Set 9

Chicken Laksa Soup

Philly Cheesesteaks

Sweet and Sour Pork Sausages

Classic Curried Mince

Chinese Lamb Steaks

Coq au Vin

Roast Pork and Amazing Crackle

# Chicken Laksa Soup

Would you love a takeaway-style laksa soup without the price tag of fast food? Slow cook it instead! The aroma of this one cooking all day is amazing. I would rate this laksa as mild to medium at most, so if you like yours hot use extra laksa paste or add some diced chilli.

**Preparation** 20 mins • **Cook** 5 hours 10 mins • **Cooker capacity** 5 litres • **Serves** 4

500 g (1 lb 2 oz) chicken breast or thigh fillets, cubed
2 cups (500 ml) chicken stock
400 ml (13½ fl oz) can light coconut milk
¼ cup laksa paste
2 tablespoons cornflour (cornstarch)
1 tablespoon minced ginger
1 tablespoon soy sauce
1 tablespoon fish sauce
1 tablespoon brown sugar
1 red onion, thinly sliced
1 red capsicum (pepper), sliced
1 tablespoon shredded kaffir lime leaves
40 g (1½ oz) vermicelli rice noodles
2 cups bean sprouts
1 cup sliced green onions/scallions/eschallots

1. Combine all the ingredients (except the noodles, bean sprouts and green onions) in the slow cooker.

2. Cover and cook on low for 5 hours.

3. Break up the noodles and add them to the slow cooker. Cover and cook for another 10 minutes or until tender.

4. Divide between serving bowls and top each bowl with bean sprouts and green onions.

# Philly Cheesesteaks

The Philly cheesesteak is a traditional street food of Philadelphia, where, as the story goes, a hotdog vender in the 1930s decided to try something new! These cheesy steak sub-style sandwiches are amazing! Imagine juicy, tasty, cheesy beef filling on your toasted rolls. Great served with French fries on the side.

**Preparation** 10 mins • **Cook** 10 hours • **Cooker capacity** 5 litres • **Serves** 8

1.25 kg (2 lb 12 oz) beef roast (see notes)
1 large brown onion, thinly sliced
1 tablespoon beef stock powder
2 teaspoons cracked black pepper
1 teaspoon garlic powder
½ teaspoon onion powder
1 tablespoon Worcestershire sauce
200 g (7 oz) gouda cheese slices (see notes)
½ cup grated mozzarella
8 extra-long crusty bread rolls, halved, lightly toasted
Butter and aioli, to taste
French fries, to serve

1. Lay the onion over the bottom of the slow cooker bowl and sit the beef on top.
2. Sprinkle with the stock powder, pepper, garlic and onion powders, and sauce.
3. Cover and cook on low for 9½ hours.
4. Transfer the beef to a cutting board and shred finely. Return the shredded beef to the slow cooker and mix with the onion and cooking juices. Cover and cook for 15 minutes, for the meat to absorb the juices.
5. Add the cheeses and continue to cook for 15 minutes, until melted, then stir through so that the melted cheese coats the steak.
6. Spread the rolls with butter and aioli, then top generously with the cheesesteak mixture. Serve piping hot with a side of French fries.

**Notes:** I use a bolar blade beef roast. Other options include sirloin, chuck roast, pot roast or brisket.

The traditional cheesesteak cheese is provolone but as that can be hard to find in Australia, I use gouda and mozzarella as the alternative. Use provolone if you can find it.

Be sure to use garlic and onion POWDER, not garlic and onion SALT. Big difference!

Some people like to add sliced mushrooms and capsicum (peppers), but I prefer this traditional version.

# Sweet and Sour Pork Sausages

This is always a hit with the young family members! These sweet and sour sausages are lovely paired with rice and Asian or stir-fried vegetables. Simple, tasty and budget friendly!

**Preparation** 20 mins • **Cook** 4–5 hours • **Cooker capacity** 6 litres • **Serves** 5

1 large brown onion, diced
1 green capsicum (pepper), diced
1 large carrot, finely diced
425 g (15 oz) can pineapple pieces in syrup
100 ml pineapple juice (or as needed)
¾ cup tomato sauce (ketchup)
⅓ cup brown sugar
2 tablespoons white vinegar
1 tablespoon soy sauce
1 teaspoon minced ginger
1 garlic clove, minced
12 thin pork sausages
Sesame seeds, to garnish
Steamed rice and vegetables, to serve

1. Combine the onion, capsicum and carrot in the slow cooker.

2. Drain the pineapple and reserve the syrup. Add the pineapple pieces to the slow cooker.

3. Pour the pineapple syrup into a measuring jug and add enough pineapple juice to make up 1 cup (250 ml) liquid. Stir in the tomato sauce, sugar, vinegar, soy, ginger and garlic.

4. Use kitchen scissors to chop the sausages into chunks (they chop very easily with scissors when raw). Add to the slow cooker then pour over the liquid mixture.

5. Cover and cook on low for 4–5 hours, stirring a couple of times during cooking.

6. Sprinkle with sesame seeds and serve with rice and more vegetables, if desired.

# Classic Curried Mince

Just like our savoury mince on page 216, this curried mince is very versatile. Use it in pies, serve it on toast, pair it with rice or vegetables – it's budget friendly and adaptable to lots of different meal types depending on whatever you feel like on the day! Our family loves it best with a simple creamy potato mash.

**Preparation** 10 mins • **Cook** 5 hours • **Cooker capacity** 5 litres • **Serves** 6

1 kg (2 lb 3 oz) minced (ground) lean beef
1 large brown onion, diced
1 large carrot, finely diced
1 heaped teaspoon minced garlic
1½ cups (375 ml) beef stock
½ cup tomato sauce (ketchup)
2 tablespoons curry powder
1 tablespoon Worcestershire sauce
1 tablespoon cornflour (cornstarch), optional

1. Combine all the ingredients (except the cornflour) in the slow cooker.

2. Cover and cook for 5 hours on low.

3. If you would like to thicken the curry, mix the cornflour with 2 tablespoons of water and stir in. Cover and cook for a further 10–15 minutes or until thickened to your liking. Season with black pepper to serve.

# Chinese Lamb Steaks

This has all the flavours of a Chinese takeaway – but it's super simple to assemble and cook with just 5 ingredients. While I used lamb steaks you could use other cuts of lamb such as chops or even shanks (though for shanks the cooking time would need to be increased to 6–7 hours.) We serve this on a bed of creamy mash, with a scattering of fresh parsley to garnish.

**Preparation** 10 mins • **Cook** 5 hours • **Cooker capacity** 5 litres • **Serves** 5

1 large onion, thinly sliced
1–1.5 kg (2 lb 3 oz–3 lb 5 oz) lamb steaks
200 g char siu sauce
1 tablespoon honey
½ teaspoon Chinese five spice
1 tablespoon cornflour (cornstarch), optional

1. Lay the onion over the bottom of the slow cooker bowl and sit the steaks on top.

2. Combine the sauce, honey and spice and pour over the steaks.

3. Cover and cook on low for 5 hours, turning steaks about halfway through cooking to get good sauce coverage.

4. If you prefer a thick sauce, mix the cornflour with 2 tablespoons water until smooth then stir into the cooking liquid for the last 30 minutes of cooking.

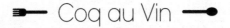
# Coq au Vin

If you are looking for something a little fancy to cook on a day you have more time – this is the recipe you want! It's a beautiful aromatic dish that is perfect for a special occasion or dinner party. Served with Dutch baby carrots and creamy potato mash, with a sprinkle of parsley to garnish, it looks amazing on the plate and tastes it too!

**Preparation** 30 mins • **Cook** 5 hours • **Cooker capacity** 6 litres • **Serves** 4

750 ml (26 fl oz) bottle red wine (I like pinot noir – see notes)
4 chicken Marylands (see notes)
2 tablespoons plain (all-purpose) flour
1 tablespoon butter
6 rashers short cut rindless bacon, cut into strips
200 g (7 oz) button mushrooms, sliced
8 small shallot onions, halved (see notes)
2 tablespoons tomato paste (concentrated puree)
½ cup (125 ml) chicken stock
2 teaspoons dried thyme
1 teaspoon dried rosemary
2 garlic cloves, minced
2 bay leaves
1 tablespoon cornflour (cornstarch)

1. Pour the wine into a saucepan on the stove and bring to the boil, uncovered. Simmer for 10–15 minutes or until reduced by half (to about 1½ cups). This gives you a more concentrated wine and reduces the alcohol content. Remove from heat and set aside.

2. Place the chicken and flour into a large plastic bag and toss to coat.

3. Melt the butter in a searing slow cooker or frying pan over high heat and cook the chicken in batches for 5 minutes, turning once, until lightly browned. If you use a pan, transfer the chicken to the slow cooker now. If you use a searing slow cooker, return it to the slow cooker setting now. Season chicken with salt and pepper.

4. Cook the bacon strips then add them to the slow cooker (or if using the searing function, before you return the chicken). The bacon can be added raw if you wish to skip the browning part.

5. Add the mushroom and eschallots to the chicken and bacon in the slow cooker.

6. In a jug, mix the reduced wine with the stock, tomato paste, thyme, rosemary and garlic. Pour this over the ingredients in the slow cooker. Add the bay leaves.

7. Cover and cook on low for 5 hours.

8. Carefully remove the chicken pieces. Place the searing slow cooker bowl onto the stovetop (or transfer contents to a saucepan). Combine the cornflour with 2 tablespoons water, stirring until smooth, and whisk into the liquid in the pan. Cook over high heat for about 5 minutes, whisking constantly, to form a thick, glossy sauce. Remove the bay leaves.

9. Pour the sauce (and the mushrooms and bacon) over the plated chicken and serve with sides and garnish.

**Notes:** Choose an inexpensive wine or one that you like to drink. You can purchase one from your bottle shop for around $5–$7. If you prefer you could choose a non-alcoholic version.

Maryland is a cut of chicken that has the thigh and drumstick attached as one large piece.

This recipe would adapt to up to 6 Marylands without further changes if you need more serves. You could also use drumsticks or thigh pieces if you prefer.

If you cannot find shallot onions (though they are available at large supermarkets), use 1 large brown onion cut into thin wedges instead.

# Roast Pork and Amazing Pork Crackle

I've never met a piece of pork rind I couldn't crackle to perfection. I'm happy to share the method for fail-proof stunning crackle every time. It's all about the salt/oil/heat balance. If you get this right you'll NEVER be disappointed in pork crackle again. Add that to beautiful juicy slow cooked pork and you have a guaranteed winner at your next roast dinner! Everyone will be talking about your crackle from that night on.

**Preparation** 15 mins • **Cook** 8½ – 9½ hours • **Cooker capacity** 5 litres • **Serves** 6

1–2 kg (2 lb 3 oz–4 lb 6 oz) boneless pork roast (any cut you prefer,
    with the rind attached)
Fine table salt
2 tablespoons oil

1. Remove any netting from the pork and place the meat directly into the slow cooker. It's okay to leave plain string on the roast but not the complex net that some pieces have around them – it's much easier to remove this net this now than at the end when it's hot and takes all your crackle with it.

2. Cover and cook on low. It will take 8 hours for 1–1.5 kg or 9 hours for 2 kg.

3. In the final 15 minutes of cooking, preheat the oven to 220°C (425°F).

4. Carefully remove the pork from the slow cooker and place it into a rimmed baking tray. Remove the string from the meat if you haven't already done so.

5. Generously apply salt all over the rind. Don't miss any spots and don't be sparing as it's important to cover it well. Using your fingertips, rub the salt all over the rind and into the scoring, but not onto the meat. The pork will be hot but usually not too hot to touch.

6. Drizzle oil over the salted rind and, again, use your fingertips to rub the oil in really well.

7. Sprinkle salt a second time over the now oily rind, but go lighter on the salt this time. Don't rub it in this time.

8. Place pork in the oven for about 30 minutes, checking it every so often to make sure it doesn't burn! The crackle is done when it's bubbled and crisp all over. I'll often tap with a carving fork to feel if it's crispy.

9. Remove carefully from oven and cut off the crackle – it will usually come away in one piece. Cut or break crackle into strips to serve. Slice the pork and serve with your favourite roast vegetables and gravy.

**Notes:** I roast vegetables in the oven for the hour or so before the pork is finished cooking. I remove them from the oven and keep them warm in their tray, covered with foil and a tea towel. Then I increase the oven temperature and cook the crackle. You can always return the veggies to the oven for the final 5 minutes to make sure they are all piping hot again. We also like to serve peas and a gravy made with a dash of the cooking juices added to boiling water and instant gravy mix.

# Notes

# Set 9 Shopping List

**MEAT**
500 g (1 lb 2 oz) chicken breast or thigh fillets
1.25 kg (2¾ lb) roast beef (I use bolar blade.
    Other options include sirloin, chuck
    roast, pot roast or brisket.)
12 thin pork sausages
1 kg (2 lb 3 oz) lean minced (ground) beef
1–1.5 kg (2 lb 3 oz–3 lb 5 oz) lamb steaks
4 chicken Marylands
6 rashers short cut rindless bacon
1–2 kg (2 lb 3 oz–4 lb 6 oz) roast pork cut of
    any kind you prefer, with the rind/crackle
    attached

**COLD PRODUCTS**
200 g (7 oz) gouda cheese slices (or
    provolone)
½ cup grated mozzarella
2 tablespoons butter

**FRESH PRODUCE**
1 red onion
4 brown onions
8 small eschallots
1 red capsicum
1 green capsicum
2 carrots
2 cups bean sprouts
1 cup sliced green onions/scallions/
    eschalots
200 g (7 oz) button mushrooms

**PANTRY**
625 ml (21 fl oz) liquid chicken stock
375 ml (12½ fl oz) liquid beef stock
400 ml (13½ fl oz) coconut milk
1 tablespoon honey
1½ tablespoons minced ginger
5 teaspoons minced garlic (or 5 fresh cloves)
2 tablespoons soy sauce (I prefer salt
    reduced)
1 tablespoon fish sauce
320 ml (11 fl oz) tomato sauce
½ teaspoons Chinese five spice
200 g (7 oz) char siu sauce
1 x 425 g (15 fl oz) pineapple chunks in syrup
100 ml (3½ fl oz) pineapple juice
2 tablespoons tomato paste (concentrated
    puree)
½ cup brown sugar
2 tablespoons white vinegar
2 tablespoons mild curry powder
3 tablespoons laksa paste
1 tablespoon shredded kaffir lime leaves
40 g (1½ oz) dried vermicelli rice noodles
1 tablespoon beef stock powder
1 teaspoons garlic powder
½ teaspoons onion powder
2 teaspoons dried thyme
1 teaspoon dried rosemary
2 bay leaves
2 tablespoons Worcestershire sauce
Aioli sauce
2 tablespoons plain flour
Table salt
2 tablespoons oil
8 long crusty long bread rolls
750 ml (26 fl oz) pinot noire
Sesame seeds
Cornflour
Cracked black pepper
Salt

# Extras

# Set 10

Creamy Smooth Vegetable Soup

Chinese Chicken

Rich Sausage Hotpot

Rainbow Frittata Slice

Classic Silverside

Moroccan Lamb Mince with Lemon Couscous
and Minted Yoghurt

Mississippi Pot Roast

# Creamy Smooth Vegetable Soup

This is a great soup to prepare at the start of the week so that you can portion and/or freeze leftovers for lunches during the week. You can omit the cream if you'd prefer a vegan version.

**Preparation** 20 mins • **Cook** 5 hours • **Cooker capacity** 6 litres • **Serves** 6

3 large potatoes, cubed
3 large carrots, cubed
1 large orange sweet potato, cubed
4 celery stalks, sliced
1 large brown onion, diced
1 large parsnip, cubed
1 tablespoon minced garlic
4 cups (1 L) vegetable stock
1 teaspoon dried thyme
300 ml (10 fl oz) cooking cream

1. Combine all the ingredients (except the cream) in the slow cooker.

2. Cover and cook on high for 5 hours or until the vegetables are fork tender.

3. Using a stick blender, blend until the soup is completely smooth.

4. Add the cream and stir through well to combine before serving.

**Note:** if you don't have a stick blender, transfer to a food processor and process until smooth.

# Chinese Chicken

This is a simple, tasty chicken recipe that doesn't need a long cooking time. Great for those days you get started a little later than usual. Serve with rice and stir-fried vegetables, or steamed greens such as broccolini and snow peas.

**Preparation** 20 mins • **Cook** 3 hours • **Cooker capacity** 3.5 litres • **Serves** 4

1 kg (2 lb 3 oz) skinless chicken thigh fillets
1 tablespoon cornflour (cornstarch)
½ cup chicken stock
¼ cup soy sauce
2 tablespoons maple syrup
2 tablespoons white wine vinegar
1 teaspoon sesame oil
¼ teaspoon smoked paprika
1 tablespoon minced garlic
2 teaspoons minced ginger
½ cup sliced green onions/scallions/eschallots
Steamed rice and vegetables, to serve
Sesame seeds and extra sliced green onions, to garnish

1. Slice the chicken into strips and place into a plastic bag with the cornflour. Toss to coat. Add the chicken to the slow cooker.

2. Combine the next 8 ingredients and pour over the chicken.

3. Cover and cook on high for 2½ hours.

4. Add the green onions then cook for a further 30 minutes, with the lid slightly ajar to help the liquid reduce and thicken. I like to use this time to cook the rice and veggies to serve with the chicken.

5. Serve sprinkled with sesame seeds and extra green onion, to garnish.

# Rich Sausage Hotpot

I originally created this recipe to take camping. We wanted something we could slow cook at home then take with us to reheat over the fire in the camp oven, but since then we cook it all the time to enjoy at home. It's just so warm and filling, and great on the budget too. Leftovers freeze well.

**Preparation** 10 mins • **Cook** 6 or 8 hours • **Cooker capacity** 6 litres • **Serves** 6–8

4–6 baby potatoes, skin on
3 carrots, sliced
1 cup frozen peas
12 thin beef sausages
400 g (14 oz) can condensed tomato soup
40 g (1½ oz) packet French onion soup mix
1 tablespoon Worcestershire sauce
½ cup warm water

1.  Cut each baby potato into 6 even-sized pieces. Add to the slow cooker along with the carrots and peas.

2.  Cut each sausage into quarters and add to the slow cooker.

3.  Combine the soup, soup mix, warm water and sauce and pour over the sausages and vegetables. Gently mix to combine.

4.  Cover and cook for 2 hours on high then 4 hours on low (equivalent to 6 hours on auto setting). You could cook on low for 8 hours if you prefer a longer cooking time.

# Rainbow Frittata Slice

I cook this vegetarian slice in a 1.5L slow cooker for a deep slice that is beautiful served in thick wedges with side salad and slaw. You can use a larger slow cooker but the slice will be much thinner so will cook faster. Whatever size cooker you use just be sure the frittata is set in the centre – if it is it will bounce back lightly when touched. You can add 150 g (5¼ oz) diced bacon to this if you don't mind it not being vegetarian.

**Preparation** 10 mins • **Cook** 2 hours • **Cooker capacity** 1.5 litres • **Serves** 4

6 eggs, whisked
1 cup grated zucchini
1 handful baby spinach leaves, sliced into thin strips
½ red onion, grated
6 cherry tomatoes, cut into quarters
125 g (4½ oz) can corn kernels, drained

1. Combine the eggs and vegetables, and season with salt and pepper.

2. Line the slow cooker with baking paper, allowing it come up the sides (this makes the slice easy to lift out and prevents sticking).

3. Pour in the egg mixture.

4. Cover, putting a tea towel (dish towel) under the lid, and cook on high for 2 hours or until set in the centre.

# Classic Silverside

If there is one thing people always seem to associate with slow cooking it's silverside. While I love all the other unique ways we cook it (for example, see page 177) I often come back to this traditional method. It's the perfect recipe to put on before work and leave unattended all day.

**Preparation** 10 mins • **Cook** 6 or 10 hours • **Cooker capacity** 6 litres • **Serves** 4–6

1 large brown onion, quartered
1.5 kg (3 lb 5 oz) piece silverside, rinsed
2 garlic cloves
4 cloves
4 black peppercorns
2 bay leaves

1. Place the onion over the bottom of the slow cooker and sit the silverside on top.

2. Add the other ingredients and enough hot water to just cover the meat.

3. Cover and cook on high for 6 hours or low for 10 hours.

# Moroccan Lamb Mince with Lemon Couscous and Minted Yoghurt Dressing

This is the perfect meal to dazzle the guests at your next dinner party, or just when you want to treat yourself and your family to a flavour fiesta! The spiced mince pairs perfectly with the lemon and mint couscous, and topped with a generous dollop of minted yoghurt dressing it's sure to please!

**Preparation** 20 mins • **Cook** 4 hours • **Cooker capacity** 3 litres • **Serves** 4

**MINTED YOGHURT DRESSING**
200 g (7 oz) tub natural yoghurt
2 teaspoons lemon juice
1 tablespoon chopped fresh mint

**MINCE**
1 kg (2 lb 3 oz) minced (ground) lamb
1 garlic clove, minced
1 red onion, diced
2 tablespoons tomato paste (concentrated puree)
1 tablespoon vegetable stock powder
40 g (1½ oz) box sultanas
400 g (14 oz) can diced tomatoes
2 teaspoons ground cumin
2 teaspoons ground coriander
2 teaspoons ground ginger
½ teaspoon cracked black pepper
½ teaspoon ground cinnamon
¼ teaspoons allspice

**LEMON COUSCOUS**
250 g (9 oz) couscous
¼ cup chopped fresh mint, plus extra leaves to garnish
Finely grated zest of 2 lemons

1. For the minted yoghurt, combine the ingredients then cover and refrigerate until meal time.

2. Add all the mince ingredients to the slow cooker.

3. Cover and cook on low for 4 hours.

4. When the mince is almost finished cooking, prepare the couscous according to the package instructions. Add the mint and lemon zest and stir to combine.

5. Serve the mince with the couscous, topped with the cool minted yoghurt and garnished with extra mint.

# Mississippi Pot Roast

After years of seeing our American members talk about this recipe, I
thoroughly enjoyed getting to try it myself! The original recipe calls
for Hidden Valley dry ranch mix, which isn't something Australian
supermarkets sell but, like me, you can easily order it online to make this
dish the way it's intended – and boy it does not disappoint! Alternatively,
you can go to page 237 for the instructions to make your own blend if
you'd prefer, as it's so easy to make! While the traditional recipe uses
pepperoncino pickled peppers, which I also couldn't get in Australia, I
substituted the mild pickled chillies that are available in our mainstream
supermarkets. I discarded them prior to serving to keep the spice level
suitable for our little ones, but by all means leave them in if you love
chillies.

**Preparation** 10 mins • **Cook** 8 hours • **Cooker capacity** 5 litres • **Serves** 4

1.5–2 kg (3 lb 5 oz–4 lb 6 oz) beef roast (blade or topside)
30 g (1 oz) sachet traditional instant gravy powder
28 g (1 oz) sachet dry ranch mix (or 30 g [1 oz] of your own home-made ranch
    mix blend, page 237)
100 g (3½ oz) butter, cubed
3 mild pickled chillies, left whole

1. Place the beef into the slow cooker. Sprinkle with the gravy powder and dry
   ranch mix.
2. Top with the butter cubes and pickled chillies.
3. Cover and cook on low for 8 hours
4. Remove and slice the roast meat, then return the slices to the gravy to coat.
5. Serve with or without the chillies, depending on your preference.

# Notes

---

---

---

---

---

---

---

---

---

---

---

---

---

---

---

---

---

# Set 10 Shopping List

## MEATS
1 kg (2 lb 3 oz) skinless chicken thigh fillets
12 thin beef sausages
1.5 g (3 lb 5 oz) corned silverside
1 kg (2 lb 3 oz) lamb mince
1.5–2 kg (3 lb 5 oz–4 lb 6 oz) beef roast
(blade or topside)

## COLD PRODUCTS
300 ml (10 fl oz) cooking cream
1 cup frozen peas
6 eggs
200 g (7 oz) tub natural yoghurt
100 g (3½ oz) butter

## FRESH PRODUCE
3 large potatoes
4–6 baby potatoes
6 large carrots
1 large orange sweet potato
4 celery stalks
2 large onions
1½ red onions
6 cherry tomatoes
1 large zucchini
Handful baby spinach leaves
1 large parsnip
¼ bunch green onions/scallions/eschalots
2 lemons
4 tablespoons chopped fresh mint

## PANTRY
4 tablespoons minced garlic
4 cups (1 L) vegetable stock
1 tablespoon vegetable stock powder
½ cup liquid chicken stock
¼ cup soy sauce (I prefer salt reduced)
2 tablespoons maple syrup
2 tablespoons white wine vinegar
1 teaspoon sesame oil
1 x 40 g (1½ oz) box sultanas
1 x 420 g (15 oz) can diced tomatoes
2 teaspoons ground cumin
2 teaspoons coriander
2 teaspoons ground ginger
½ teaspoons cinnamon
¼ teaspoons allspice
1 teaspoon dried thyme
¼ teaspoons smoked paprika
2 teaspoons minced ginger
sesame seeds, to garnish
1 x 30 g (1 oz) sachet traditional instant gravy
mix
1 x 28 g (1 oz) sachet dry ranch mix (or make
your own; see page 237)
1 tablespoon Worcestershire sauce
125 g (4½ oz) can corn kernels
1 x 400 g (14 oz) can condensed tomato
soup
1 x 40 g (1½ oz) sachet dry French onion
soup mix
4 whole cloves
4 whole peppercorns
2 bay leaves
2 tablespoons tomato paste (concentrated
puree)
250 g (9 oz) couscous
3 mild pickled chillies
Cornflour
Cracked black pepper
Salt

# Extras

# Set 11

Chinese Chicken Noodle and Sweetcorn Soup

Honey Soy Pork Rashers

Cheesy Chicken and Broccoli Pasta

Chilli Con Carne

Honey Mustard Chicken

Beef Cheeks in Guinness Gravy

Classic Roast Lamb

# Chinese Chicken Noodle and Sweetcorn Soup

This is a classic chicken and corn soup with a Chinese twist.

**Preparation** 15 mins • **Cook** 5 hours 10 minutes• **Cooker capacity** 5 litres • **Serves** 4

4 cups chicken stock
4 skinless chicken thigh fillets
420 g (15 oz) can corn kernels, drained
420 g (15 oz) can creamed corn
1 tablespoon minced ginger
1 tablespoon minced garlic
2 tablespoons soy sauce
2 teaspoons sesame oil
2 eggs, whisked
75 g (2½ oz) packet 2-minute noodles (no seasoning added)
1 cup sliced green onions/scallions/eschallots, plus extra to garnish

1. Add all the ingredients (except the eggs, noodles and green onions) to the slow cooker.
2. Cover and cook on low for 5 hours.
3. Remove the chicken, shred finely and return to the slow cooker.
4. Whisk the soup, then while whisking pour in the eggs to create ribbons of whisked egg throughout the soup.
5. Add the noodles and green onions. Cover and cook for a further 10 minutes.
6. Serve garnished with extra green onions.

# Honey Soy Pork Rashers

This yummy honey and soy combo is perfect on pork rashers. If you are unsure what pork rashers are, ask your local friendly butcher. As a tip, they look like slices of pork belly. Look for thick cut, narrow slices with rind on the edge. We serve ours with sweet potato fries and a crispy side salad.

**Preparation** 10 mins • **Cook** 3½ hours • **Cooker capacity** 5 litres • **Serves** 5

12 pork rashers (1 kg/2 lb 3 oz)
⅔ cup honey
⅓ cup soy sauce
¼ cup Chinese cooking wine
1 tablespoon sesame oil
1 tablespoon minced ginger
2 teaspoons minced garlic

1. Lay the pork rashers into the slow cooker.

2. Combine all the other ingredients and pour over the pork.

3. Cover and cook on high for 3½ hours, turning halfway through the cooking time, if possible, for rich colour on both sides. Remove rashers from cooking liquid and serve immediately.

# Cheesy Chicken and Broccoli Pasta

This classic flavour combination is perfect in your slow cooker. It's a firm favourite with kids of all ages in our house. Time saving tip: This recipe uses cooked pasta, but you could pre-cook your pasta in the morning to make it a simple one pot slow cooker meal later on in the day. Simply cook and drain your pasta then toss it with a little oil and store it in a sealed container in the fridge until the evening. Just before adding it to your slow cooker run it under hot tap water in a strainer to bring it back up to a just-cooked temperature.

**Preparation** 20 mins • **Cook** 3 hours 50 mins • **Cooker capacity** 5 litres • **Serves** 5

500 g (1 lb 2 oz) skinless chicken thigh fillets
1 cup (250 ml) chicken stock
2 garlic cloves, minced
300 g (10½ oz) frozen broccoli florets
300 g (10½ oz) sour cream
2 tablespoons wholegrain mustard
50 g (1¾ oz) semi-dried tomatoes, chopped
6 green onions/scallions/eschallots, sliced
350 g (12½ oz) rigatoni, cooked to al dente
½ cup grated parmesan
½ cup grated mozzarella

1. Combine the chicken, stock and garlic in the slow cooker.
2. Cover and cook on low for 3 hours, then add the broccoli and cook for a further 30 minutes.
3. Drain the liquid from the slow cooker. Remove the chicken, shred, then return it to the broccoli in the slow cooker.
4. Add the sour cream, mustard, tomatoes, green onions and hot cooked pasta to the slow cooker. Mix gently to combine.
5. Top with the cheeses. Cover and cook for a further 20 minutes to melt the cheeses and heat all ingredients through.

# Chilli Con Carne

There is just something about a big bowl of warming chilli on a cold night. You could even serve it on crunchy corn chips, nachos-style! I always like to add just a little dark chocolate to mine to take it to the next level of taste – try it and you won't regret it. This recipe has a medium heat spice level so feel free to adjust the chilli powder to your preference.

**Preparation** 15 mins • **Cook** 5 hours • **Cooker capacity** 6 litres • **Serves** 6

1.5 kg (3 lb 5 oz) minced (ground) beef
1 large red capsicum (pepper), diced
1 large brown onion, diced
2 x 400 g (14 oz) cans diced tomatoes
400 g (14 oz) can red kidney beans, drained and rinsed
¼ cup tomato paste (concentrated puree)
2 tablespoons ground cumin
1 tablespoon garlic powder
1 tablespoon beef stock powder
2 teaspoons ground chilli powder
4 squares good-quality dark chocolate
Corn chips and sour cream, to serve

1. Combine all the ingredients (except chocolate) in the slow cooker.

2. Cover and cook on low for 5 hours, stirring occasionally to break down any mince lumps (I like to use a potato masher for a fine texture).

3. Place the chocolate on top, cover and stand for 5 minutes to melt. Stir through well.

4. Serve with corn chips and a good dollop of sour cream.

# Honey Mustard Chicken with Bacon

This chicken dish has a lovely family-friendly flavour everyone will enjoy. Serve with rice and green salad or mashed potato and steamed vegetables.

**Preparation** 15 mins • **Cook** 4 hours • **Cooker capacity** 5 litres • **Serves** 4

1 kg (2 lb 3 oz) skinless chicken pieces (thigh fillets or 8 lovely leg drumsticks)
100 g (3½ oz) diced bacon
420 g (15 oz) can condensed cream of chicken soup
2 garlic cloves, minced
⅓ cup honey
2 tablespoons wholegrain mustard

1. Place the chicken and bacon into the slow cooker.

2. Combine all the other ingredients and pour over the chicken.

3. Cover and cook on low for 4 hours.

# Beef Cheeks in Guinness Gravy

This recipe was my first experience of cooking beef cheeks. The cut has received so much attention in recent years that I wanted to explore it too – and I'm so glad I did. My 18 year old son told me 'It's the best thing I've eaten in months!' so I'm going to say it was a success. Our family all enjoyed it with cheesy potato and chive mash and steamed broccolini.

**Preparation** 15 mins • **Cook** 6 hours • **Cooker capacity** 6 litres • **Serves** 4

4 beef cheeks
¼ cup plain (all-purpose) flour
1 tablespoon beef stock powder
½ teaspoon cracked black pepper
2 carrots, sliced
2 celery stalks, sliced
1 brown onion, diced
2 garlic cloves, minced
250 ml (9 fl oz) Guinness (dark stout)
¼ cup tomato paste (concentrated puree)
1 tablespoon brown sugar
2 teaspoons dried thyme
2 teaspoons dried parsley

1. Place the beef, flour, stock powder and pepper in a large plastic bag and shake to coat the beef well.

2. Spread the carrots, celery and onion over the bottom of the slow cooker then sit the cheeks on top.

3. Combine the remaining ingredients and pour over.

4. Cover and cook on low for 6 hours. There's no need to turn the beef during cooking.

5. Gently transfer one beef cheek to each plate. Using a slotted spoon top the beef with the vegetables, then spoon over the gravy.

# Classic Roast Lamb

Nothing beats classic, tender, slow cooked roast lamb. The garlic and rosemary lift this meal to the taste heavens! Serve with your favourite roast vegetables and gravy for a lush Sunday roast dinner.

**Preparation** 15 mins • **Cook** 8 hours • **Cooker capacity** 6 litres • **Serves** 6

1.5 kg (3 lb 5 oz) boneless lamb leg or shoulder roast
4 garlic cloves, halved lengthways
8 x 3 cm (1 inch) sprigs fresh rosemary
½ cup hot water
1–2 tablespoons mint sauce (or 4 mint leaves, thinly sliced)
2 teaspoons beef stock powder
Gravy powder or granules, optional

1. Using a small sharp knife, make 8 small slits, about 2 cm (¾ inch) in length and depth, over the upper surface of the lamb. Insert half a garlic clove and a sprig of rosemary into each slit (it's okay if the rosemary sticks out a little from each one).

2. Transfer the lamb to the slow cooker.

3. Put the hot water, mint sauce and stock powder in a bowl or jug. Stir to combine then gently pour over the lamb.

4. Cover and cook on low for 8 hours, occasionally spooning the cooking juices over the lamb if you are around to do so.

5. Transfer the cooked lamb to a cutting board. Remove and discard the garlic and rosemary pieces. Cover loosely with foil and set aside to rest for 5–10 minutes.

6. If you would like to make gravy, combine the gravy powder or granules with pan juices in a small saucepan and cook over high heat on the stovetop until thickened.

7. Carve the roast in thick slices (easier than thin when it's extra tender like this), and serve with gravy and vegetables.

# Notes

# Set 11 Shopping List

## MEAT

500 g (1 lb 2 oz) + 4 skinless chicken thigh
   fillets
12 pork rashers (approx. 1 kg [2 lb 3 oz])
1.5 kg (3 lb 5 oz) minced (ground) beef
1 kg (2 lb 3 oz) boneless, skinless chicken
   pieces (eg thigh fillets or 8 lovely leg
   drumsticks)
100 g (3½ oz) diced bacon
4 beef cheeks
1.5 g (3 lb 5 oz) boneless lamb leg or
   shoulder roast

## COLD PRODUCTS

2 eggs
300 g (10½ oz) frozen broccoli florets
300 g (10½ oz) sour cream
50 g (1¾ oz) semidried tomatoes, chopped
½ cup grated parmesan cheese
½ cup grated mozzarella cheese
1 small tub sour cream
8 sprigs fresh rosemary

## FRESH PRODUCE

1 bunch green onions/scallions/eschallots
1 red capsicum
2 onions
2 carrots
2 stalks celery
4 cloves fresh garlic

## PANTRY

1.25 litres (2.6 pints) liquid chicken stock
4 tablespoons beef stock powder
420 g (13 oz) can corn kernels
420 g (13 oz) can creamed corn
2 tablespoons minced ginger
4 tablespoons minced garlic
2 tablespoons sesame oil
1 x 75 g (2¾ oz) packet 2 minute noodles
½ cup soy sauce
1 cup honey
¼ cup Chinese cooking wine
4 tablespoons wholegrain mustard
350 g (12½ oz) rigatoni
2 x 400 g (14 oz) cans diced tomatoes
1 x 400 g (14 oz) can red kidney beans
1 x 420 g (15 oz) can condensed cream of
   chicken soup
½ cup tomato paste (tomato concentrate)
2 teaspoons ground chilli powder
2 tablespoons ground cumin
1 tablespoon garlic powder
2 teaspoons dried thyme
2 teaspoons dried parsley
4 squares good quality strong dark chocolate
Corn chips, to serve
¼ cup plain flour
250 ml (9 fl oz) dark stout beer
1 tablespoon brown sugar
1–2 tablespoons mint sauce (or 4 mint
   leaves)
1 sachet instant gravy mix, roast meat style
Cornflour
Cracked black pepper
Salt

# Extras

# Set 12

Minestrone Soup

Silverside in Soft Drink

Lemongrass Chicken

Carolina BBQ Pork Chops

Sweet Chilli BBQ Whole Chicken

Oriental Beef Lettuce Bowls

Pork Belly in Apple Cider

# Minestrone Soup

This is a hearty filling vegetarian soup that's great for large appetites – plus you can portion up any leftovers for easy meals later in the week. Serve with buttered crusty bread stick slices or a scattering of crispy croutons.

**Preparation** 20 mins • **Cook** 9 hours • **Cooker capacity** 6 litres • **Serves** 8–10

4 cups (1 L) vegetable stock
800 g (1 lb 12 oz) can diced Italian tomatoes
400 g (14 oz) can cannellini beans, drained and rinsed
3 potatoes, skin on, cut into 1 cm (⅓ inch) cubes
4 celery stalks, sliced
3 carrots, cut into 1 cm (⅓ inch) cubes
2 large brown onions, diced
Large handful of green beans, coarsely chopped
⅓ cup tomato paste (concentrated puree)
2 tablespoons fresh basil, sliced
1 tablespoon minced garlic
2 teaspoons dried oregano
2 teaspoons dried thyme
½ teaspoon salt
1 teaspoon cracked black pepper
1 large zucchini, cut into 1 cm (⅓ inch) cubes
100 g (3½ oz) baby spinach leaves
½ cup macaroni

1. Combine all the ingredients (except the zucchini, spinach and macaroni) in the slow cooker.
2. Cover and cook on low for 8 hours.
3. Add the last 3 ingredients. Cover and cook for a further 1 hour, or until the pasta is tender.

# Silverside in Soft Drink

When you want to try something different from your classic silverside (page 156) try this! It all began with ginger beer, then we moved on to lemonade and even sparkling mineral water with some fresh lemon and lime wedges. Sparkling apple juice is also good. You can use either the full sugar or diet version of the drinks. It's the carbonation that tenderises the meat, and the drink also brings just the hint of flavour you need. Ginger beer (or ginger ale for a slightly milder taste) is my absolute favourite, and I don't even like the drink itself – that's how mild and complementary the flavour is.

**Preparation** 5 mins • **Cook** 8–10 low or 5–6 hours high • **Cooker capacity** 6 litres • **Serves** 6

> 1–2 kg (2 lb 3 oz–4 lb 6 oz) piece silverside
> 5 cups (1.25 L) bubbly soft drink (soda) of your choice

1. Rinse the silverside and place into the slow cooker.
2. Pour over the soft drink – it doesn't have to fully cover the meat.
3. Cover and cook on low for 8–10 hours or high for 5–6 hours, turning the meat halfway through cooking if possible.

**Note:** Use the weight of meat that will suit your family best, but don't forget there are many ways to use up leftovers, which will keep in the fridge for up to 4 days.

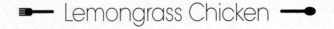

# Lemongrass Chicken

This recipe has an amazing flavour, but there's more – the aromatic lemongrass will fill your house with the most incredible, beautiful citrus notes while it cooks! We like to serve it with jasmine rice and an Asian vegetable stir-fry mix like carrot, baby corn, broccoli, beans and bamboo shoots.

**Preparation** 15 mins • **Cook** 5 hours • **Cooker capacity** 6 litres • **Serves** 5

1–2 lemongrass stalks (1 is fine but 2 will give even more flavour)
10 chicken thigh cutlets (bone in, skin on)
1 brown onion, thinly sliced
3 garlic cloves, minced
1 teaspoon minced ginger
1 tablespoon fish sauce
1 tablespoon fresh lime juice
2 teaspoons soy sauce
2 tablespoons brown sugar

1. To prepare the lemongrass, remove the tough outer layers and trim the stalk – you will use only the white and very pale green part. Slice finely and spread over the bottom of the slow cooker.

2. Sit the chicken thighs on top of the lemongrass. Scatter the onion over.

3. Combine the garlic, ginger, fish sauce, lime juice, soy sauce and brown sugar in a jug, and pour over the chicken.

4. Cover and cook on low for 5 hours.

5. The chicken will release lots of liquid as it cooks. About halfway through the cooking time, spoon the liquid over the chicken so it blends with the other sauce ingredients.

6. To serve, lift the chicken from the slow cooker and discard the cooking liquid.

# Carolina BBQ Pork Chops

While I have used pork chops for this recipe, you could add the same flavours to pork ribs or pork fillet. The flavour is delicious and very adaptable. We serve it with beer battered steakhouse chips and freshly made slaw.

**Preparation** 10 mins • **Cook** 3½ hours • **Cooker capacity** 5 litres • **Serves** 6

6 pork chops, excess fat removed
½ cup yellow mustard
¼ cup brown sugar
¼ apple cider vinegar
2 tablespoons tomato sauce (ketchup)
1 teaspoon Worcestershire sauce
1 teaspoon garlic powder

1. Place the chops into the slow cooker.

2. Combine all the other ingredients and pour over the pork.

3. Cover and cook on low for 3½ hours, turning the chops halfway through the cooking time to coat them nicely in the sauce.

**Note:** If the pork chops are very thick they may need a longer cooking time. After 3½ hours, check and cook longer if necessary, checking every 15–30 minutes until tender.

# Sweet Chilli BBQ Whole Chicken

Don't let the simple ingredients fool you, this is loaded with flavour and who doesn't like an easy to prepare dinner! Serve the chicken with salad in summer or with roast vegetables in the cooler months. If you have any leftover chicken it's great on salad wraps the next day for lunch. Turn to pages 18–19 for tips on cooking a whole chicken.

**Preparation** 15 mins • **Cook** 7 hours • **Cooker capacity** 6 litres • **Serves** 4

1 small brown onion, peeled
1 whole chicken (about 2 kg/4 lb 6 oz)
½ cup BBQ sauce
⅓ cup sweet chilli sauce
1 teaspoon minced garlic
1 teaspoon minced ginger

1. Place the onion inside the chicken cavity, then place the chicken into the slow cooker.
2. Combine the other ingredients and pour over the chicken.
3. Cover and cook on low for 7 hours, basting with cooking juices several times during cooking for a richer colour.

# Oriental Beef Lettuce Bowls

This is a similar concept to a san choy bow but using beef mince. We like to serve ours on long cos lettuce leaves, but you use iceberg lettuce cups instead. Where possible choose lean beef over regular beef to keep the oil content down in the final dish. The garnish keeps it looking fresh and fancy and it makes a beautiful entrée or main for your next dinner party with minimal effort!

**Preparation** 15 mins • **Cook** 3½ hours • **Cooker capacity** 3.5 litres • **Serves** 5

500 g (1 lb 2 oz) minced (ground) lean beef
1 carrot, grated
2 small shallot onions, finely diced
2 garlic cloves, minced
2 teaspoons minced ginger
¼ cup soy sauce
1 tablespoon mirin
2 teaspoons sesame oil
2 tablespoons brown sugar
1 tablespoon sesame seeds, plus 1 teaspoon extra to garnish
3 green onions/scallions/eschallots, sliced, plus 1 extra, sliced, to garnish
10 cos lettuce leaves
1 red chilli, deseeded and finely sliced, to garnish

1. Combine the mince, carrot, diced shallot onions, garlic, ginger, soy sauce, mirin, sesame oil and sugar in the slow cooker. Mix well.

2. Cover and cook on low for 3½ hours, stirring through the sesame seeds and green onions for the final 15 minutes of cooking.

3. Using a slotted spoon, scoop the mixture from the slow cooker into the lettuce leaves (discard the excess liquid).

4. Serve garnished with extra sesame seeds and green onions, and the chilli.

# Pork Belly with Apple Cider

Beautiful pork belly with hints of apple sweetness, and crispy delicious crackle! This meat is moist and tender, and delicious served with gravy and roasted vegetables.

**Preparation** 15 mins • **Cook** 6 hours 30 mins • **Cooker capacity** 6 litres • **Serves** 4–6

1 large brown onion, chopped
1 large green apple, cored and chopped
1 leek, sliced
2 teaspoons chicken stock powder
1 teaspoon dried thyme
330 ml (11 fl oz) bottle apple cider (we use non-alcoholic but either is fine)
1 kg (2 lb 3 oz) piece pork belly, rind scored
Fine table salt
2 tablespoons oil

1. Add the onion, apple, leek, stock and thyme to the slow cooker then pour over the cider. Sit pork on top.

2. Cover and cook on low for 6 hours. In the final 15 minutes of cooking time, preheat the oven to 220°C (425°F).

3. Carefully remove the pork belly from the slow cooker and place it, rind side up, onto a rimmed oven tray.

4. Generously sprinkle salt all over the rind, without leaving any gaps. Don't be sparing on the salt as it's important to cover it well. Using your fingertips, rub the salt all over the rind and into the scoring, but not onto the meat. The pork will be hot but is not usually too hot to touch.

5. Drizzle the oil over the salted rind and, again, use your fingertips to rub it in really well.

6. Sprinkle salt a second time over the now oily rind, but go lighter on the salt this time. Don't rub it in this time.

7. Place the pork into the oven and cook for 20–30 minutes, checking it every so often to make sure it doesn't burn, until the crackle is bubbly and crisp.

8. Cut into portions and serve with gravy and your choice of vegetables.

# Notes

# Set 12 Shopping List

## MEATS
1–2 kg (2 lb 3 oz–4 lb 6 oz) piece corned
    silverside
10 chicken thigh cutlets (bone in, skin on)
6 medium pork chops
1 whole chicken
500 g (1 lb 2 oz) minced (ground) lean beef
1 kg (2 lb 3 oz) piece pork belly

## FRESH PRODUCE
3 medium potatoes
4 celery stalks
4 carrots
5 onions
2 small eschallots
1 zucchini
1 lime
1 large green apple
1 leek
1 large handful of green beans
2 tablespoons fresh basil
100 g (3½ oz) baby spinach leaves
1–2 lemongrass stalks
4 green onions/scallions/eschalots
1 large cos lettuce
1 red chilli

## PANTRY
1 litre (2 pints) liquid vegetable stock
2 teaspoons chicken stock powder
800 g (1 lb 12 oz) can diced Italian tomatoes
400 g (14 oz) can cannellini beans
⅓ cup tomato paste (concentrated puree)
4 tablespoons minced garlic
4 teaspoons minced ginger
4 tablespoons soy sauce (I prefer salt
    reduced)
2 teaspoons dried oregano
3 teaspoons dried thyme
1 teaspoon garlic powder
½ cup macaroni
1.25 litre (42 fl oz) bottle ginger beer (or soft
    drink of your choice) for silverside
1 tablespoon fish sauce
½ cup brown sugar
½ cup yellow mustard
¼ apple cider vinegar
2 tablespoons tomato sauce (ketchup)
1 teaspoon Worcestershire sauce
½ cup BBQ sauce
⅓ cup sweet chilli sauce
1 tablespoons mirin
2 tablespoons brown sugar
2 teaspoons sesame oil
1½ tablespoons sesame seeds
1 x 330 ml (11 fl oz) bottle apple cider (we
    use non-alcoholic but either is fine)
Fine table salt
2 tablespoons oil
Cornflour
Cracked black pepper
Salt

# Extras

# Set 13

Zesty Tomato Soup

Apricot Chicken

Honey Soy Sausages

Pesto Chicken and Broccoli

Rissoles in Streaky Bacon Sauce

Massaman Lamb Shanks with Potatoes and Green Beans

Mustard Maple Roast Lamb

#  Zesty Tomato Soup

This fresh, made-from-scratch tomato soup is simply mouth-watering! You can make it creamy or omit the cream if you prefer. See notes below for vegetarian options.

**Preparation** 15 mins • **Cook** 5 hours • **Cooker capacity** 3 litres • **Serves** 4

2 x 400 g (14 oz) cans diced tomatoes
500 ml (17 fl oz) salt-reduced chicken stock (see note)
1 brown onion, finely diced
1 celery stalk, finely diced
1 teaspoon cracked black pepper
¼ cup fresh basil leaves, finely sliced (see note), plus extra fresh basil leaves to garnish
2 garlic cloves, minced
2 tablespoons brown sugar
200 ml (6¾ fl oz) cooking cream
Crusty bread, to serve

1. Combine all the ingredients (except the cream) in the slow cooker.
2. Cover and cook on high for 5 hours.
3. Stir through the cooking cream, then use a stick blender to blend until smooth.
4. Serve garnished with basil leaves, with crusty bread.

**Note:** Chicken stock could be swapped out for vegetable stock to create a vegetarian friendly version (and omitting the cream will make it vegan). You could use dried basil, but reduce the amount to 1½ tablespoons.

#  Apricot Chicken

This is such a classic recipe and another firm favourite of my childhood! While my mum cooked hers on the stovetop or microwave, naturally I slow cook mine. This recipe uses thigh fillets, but it also works with breast fillets, drumsticks, thigh cutlets or wings. If using bone-in pieces increase the cooking time by an hour. Serve with rice or mashed potato and vegetables.

**Preparation** 10 mins • **Cook** 4 hours • **Cooker capacity** 5 litres • **Serves** 4

1 kg (2 lb 3 oz) skinless chicken thigh fillets
1 onion, diced
40 g (1½ oz) packet dry French onion soup mix
425 ml (14 ½ fl oz) can apricot nectar

1. Place the chicken and the onion into the slow cooker.

2. Combine the soup mix and nectar and pour over the chicken.

3. Cover and cook on low for 4 hours.

**Note:** You could add 1–2 teaspoons curry powder to this recipe to make apricot chicken curry.

# Honey Soy Sausages

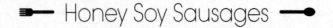

These sausage bites are great served with rice, pasta or vegetables. You can also serve them on toothpicks for party nibbles in a perfect mouthful!

**Preparation** 10 mins • **Cook** 4 hours • **Cooker capacity** 3.5 litres • **Serves** 5

10 chicken sausages
½ cup kecap manis (sweet soy sauce)
½ cup honey
1 tablespoon hot water
1 tablespoon sesame seeds, plus extra to garnish, optional

1. Using kitchen scissors, chop the raw sausages into bite-sized pieces. Place into the slow cooker.

2. Combine all the other ingredients and pour over the sausages.

3. Cover and cook on low for 4 hours. Initially the liquid will be quite thick, so after the first 30 minutes of cooking when it has warmed up, toss the sausages through the sauce to coat.

4. Use a slotted spoon to lift the sausages from the slow cooker, and discard the cooking liquid. Garnish with extra sesame seeds if you like.

# Pesto Chicken and Broccoli

This cheesy, creamy chicken and broccoli is amazing with the flavours of basil pesto throughout. A hit with all ages! We serve it with creamy potato mash and julienned carrots. Another option would be to serve it over penne or rice.

**Preparation** 10 mins • **Cook** 4 hours • **Cooker capacity** 5 litres • **Serves** 5

4 large chicken breast fillets, cut into large chunks
500 g (1 lb 2 oz) broccoli, cut into florets
300 ml (10 fl oz) cooking cream
3 garlic cloves, minced
190 g (6½ oz) jar basil pesto
1 tablespoon cornflour (cornstarch), optional
250 g (9 oz) grated cheese (see note)

1. Place the chicken and broccoli into the slow cooker.

2. Combine the cream with the garlic and pesto and pour over the chicken. Mix gently to combine.

3. Cover, putting a tea towel (dish towel) under the lid, and cook on low for 3½ hours.

4. If you plan to thicken the sauce (see note), mix the cornflour with 2 tablespoons water until smooth, then stir into the chicken mixture. Sprinkle the grated cheese on top, cover and cook for a further 30 minutes to thicken the sauce and melt the cheese. If you don't use the cornflour, just sprinkle with cheese, cover and cook for 30 minutes, to melt.

**Notes:** When serving this with vegetables I like to thicken the sauce before adding the cheese. However, if you are serving it on rice or pasta you may prefer to skip this step for a saucier topping.

For the grated cheese I like a cheddar, mozzarella and pecorino blend. You can mix the cheeses yourself to make up the amount, or buy them already mixed. If you only have one type of cheese that's okay too – use any grated cheese you like.

# Rissoles in Streaky Bacon Sauce

We serve these rissoles with creamy mashed potato and peas, and a generous ladle of the chunky bacon tomato sauce over the top – so good! A great option is to prepare this ahead of time – sit the rissoles in the fridge on a covered plate and the rest of the ingredients in a bowl (also covered) in the fridge, then simply add everything to the slow cooker later in the day when you are ready to cook.

**Preparation** 20 mins • **Cook** 5 hours • **Cooker capacity** 6 litres • **Makes** 16 medium rissoles

### RISSOLES
500 g (1 lb 2 oz) minced (ground) lean beef
500 g (1 lb 2 oz) sausage mince
1 cup packaged dried breadcrumbs
½ cup finely grated parmesan
1 egg

### SAUCE
350 g (12½ oz) streaky bacon, coarsely diced
1 small brown onion, finely diced
2 garlic cloves, minced
2 cups passata (pureed tomato sauce)
¼ cup brown sugar
¼ cup white vinegar
1 tablespoon Worcestershire sauce
1 teaspoon smoked paprika
1 teaspoon mustard powder

1. Place all rissole ingredients into a large bowl and season with salt and pepper. Use your hands to combine. I like to wear disposable gloves for rissole making as it means so much less mess!

2. Roll the meat mixture into 16 balls the size of the centre of your palm, then flatten each one slightly.

3. Place the rissoles into the slow cooker as you go. Make a single layer if your slow cooker allows you to, or overlap slightly.

4. Combine all the sauce ingredients and pour over rissoles.

5. Cover, putting a tea towel (dish towel) under the lid, and cook on low for 5 hours.

6. If you are around to turn them over halfway, do so gently. They'll hold together nicely by this time.

7. Just before serving you may notice some oil has risen to the top of the sauce. Scoop this out and discard before serving.

8. Serve rissoles generously topped with the sauce.

# Massaman Lamb Shanks with Potatoes and Green Beans

This is a hearty one pot dinner that can be put on to cook in the morning and left alone until dinner time. Perfect for a long work day or a busy weekend day! The aromas while cooking will make you the envy of your street. I keep the spice level mild in this so the whole family can enjoy it. My 'I don't really like curries' husband even looks for seconds as the flavours are amazing!

**Preparation** 15 mins • **Cook** 8 hours • **Cooker capacity** 6 litres • **Serves** 4

4 lamb shanks
400 g (14 oz) potatoes, cut into chunky (about 1 inch) cubes
1 brown onion, roughly diced
250 g (9 oz) green beans, topped and halved
100 g Massaman curry paste
400 ml (13½ fl oz) can coconut cream
1 tablespoon fish sauce
1 tablespoon brown sugar
1 tablespoon lime juice
Fresh coriander leaves, to garnish

1. Place the lamb shanks into the slow cooker and arrange the potatoes around them. You want the potatoes down low so the sauce covers them during cooking.

2. Top with the onion and beans.

3. Combine the curry paste, coconut cream, fish sauce, sugar and lime juice and pour over.

4. Cover and cook on low for 8 hours.

5. Gently transfer the lamb shanks to serving plates (they will be very tender so support their weight as you lift them so they don't fall off the bone).

6. Top with the vegetables and pour over plenty of the sauce.

7. Garnish generously with fresh coriander.

# Mustard Maple Roast Lamb

This beautiful tender roast lamb will absolutely melt in your mouth! We serve it with mashed potato and steamed veggies, and a drizzle of our favourite roast meat gravy. We've never had leftovers as everyone goes back for seconds until it's all gone!

**Preparation** 10 mins • **Cook** 9 hours • **Cooker capacity** 5 litres • **Serves** 6

5 palm-length sprigs fresh rosemary
1.5–2 kg (3 lb 5 oz–4 lb 6 oz) boneless lamb leg or shoulder roast
⅓ cup maple syrup
⅓ cup red wine (I use a non-alcoholic cooking wine)
1 tablespoon Dijon mustard
1 tablespoon minced garlic

1.  Place the rosemary over the bottom of the slow cooker and sit the lamb on top.

2.  Combine the remaining ingredients and pour over the lamb.

3.  Cover and cook on low for 9 hours, basting occasionally with the cooking juices for maximum flavour.

4.  Remove the lamb from the slow cooker and slice or shred the meat, to enjoy with your favourite veggies and gravy.

# Notes

# Set 13 Shopping List

**MEATS**
1 kg (2 lb 3 oz) chicken thigh fillets
10 chicken sausages
4 large chicken breasts
500 g (1 lb 2 oz) minced (ground) lean beef
500 g (1 lb 2 oz) sausage mince
350 g (12½ oz) streaky bacon
4 lamb shanks
1.5–2 kg (3 lb 5 oz–4 lb 6 oz) boneless lamb
    leg or shoulder roast

**COLD PRODUCTS**
500 ml (17 fl oz) cooking cream
250 g (9 oz) grated cheese (I like a cheddar,
    mozzarella and pecorino blend)
½ cup finely grated parmesan cheese
1 egg

**FRESH PRODUCE**
4 onions
1 stalk celery
⅓ cup fresh basil
2 cups broccoli florets (or 500 g frozen
    broccoli)
400 g (14 oz) potatoes
250 g (9 oz) green beans
1 lime
¼ bunch coriander
5 palm-length sprigs fresh rosemary

**PANTRY**
2 x 400 g (14 oz) cans peeled diced tomato
500 ml (17 fl oz) reduced salt chicken stock
4–5 tablespoons minced garlic
⅔ cup brown sugar
1 x 40 sachet dry French onion soup mix
425 ml (14½ fl oz) can apricot nectar
½ cup kecap manis (sweet soy sauce)
½ cup honey
1 tablespoon sesame seeds
⅓ cup maple syrup
⅓ cup red wine (we use the non-alcoholic
    cooking kind)
1 tablespoon Dijon mustard
190 g jar basil pesto
1 cup packaged dried breadcrumbs
2 cups passata (pureed tomato)
1 teaspoons smoked paprika
¼ cup white vinegar
1 teaspoons mustard powder
1 tablespoon Worcestershire sauce
100 g (3½ oz) Massaman curry paste
400 ml (13½ fl oz) coconut cream
1 tablespoon fish sauce
Cornflour
Cracked black pepper
Salt

# Extras

# Set 14

Creamy Potato and Bacon Soup

Chicken Slaw Salad

Beautiful Brisket Shredded

Mango Coconut Curried Sausages

Satay Pulled Pork Poutine

Mexican Stuffed Capsicums

Complete Roast Beef Dinner

# Creamy Potato and Bacon Soup

This cheesy potato soup is a filling and delicious soup the whole family will enjoy. Garnish it with green onions, crispy bacon pieces and extra cheese, and serve it with your favourite crusty bread ready to dip in – Turkish pide bread is a favourite of ours with this soup.

**Preparation** 20 mins • **Cook** 5 hours 20 mins • **Cooker capacity** 6 litres • **Serves** 6

1.2 kg (2 lb 10 oz) potatoes, diced
1 large brown onion, diced
6 cups (1.5 L) chicken stock
¼ teaspoon salt
½ teaspoon cracked black pepper
200 g (7 oz) diced bacon
300 ml (10 fl oz) milk
300 ml (10 fl oz) cooking cream
1 tablespoon cornflour (cornstarch)
2 cups grated tasty cheese
200 g (7 oz) diced bacon, extra, to serve
½ cup sliced green onions/scallions/eschallots, to serve
1 cup grated tasty cheese, extra, to serve

1. Combine the potatoes, onion, stock, salt, pepper and 200 g bacon in the slow cooker.

2. Cover and cook on high for 5 hours.

3. Mix the cornflour with 2 tablespoons of the milk until smooth, then mix in the cream and remaining milk. Stir this into the soup, along with the grated cheese. Cook, covered, for a further 20 minutes until the cheese has melted.

4. Cook the extra bacon in a frying pan until crisp. Divide the soup among serving bowls and garnish with crispy bacon, green onions and extra cheese.

# Chicken Slaw Salad

This makes an amazing fresh chicken salad mix. We have it for dinner on tortilla wraps with lettuce, then I have enough left over for another two days' worth of school and work lunch sandwich fillings. Fresh, crunchy salad with shredded chicken in a creamy dressing!

**Preparation** 20 mins • **Cook** 5 hours **Cooker capacity** 5 litres
• **Makes** 15+ sandwiches or wraps

4 large skinless chicken breast fillets
2 cups chicken stock
2 celery stalks, diced
½ red capsicum (pepper), diced
½ green capsicum (pepper), diced
1 large carrot, grated
3 green onions/scallions/eschallots, finely sliced
½ red onion, diced
2 x 125 g (4½ oz) cans corn kernels, drained
1 tomato, diced
1 cup low-fat mayonnaise
½ cup light sour cream
1 teaspoon wholegrain mustard

1. Place the whole chicken breasts and stock into the slow cooker and season with salt and pepper.

2. Cover and cook on low for 5 hours.

3. Remove the chicken from the cooking liquid and shred into thin strips with two forks.

4. Place the shredded chicken into a large mixing bowl.

5. Add the remaining ingredients and mix well to combine.

**Notes:** The salad will keep refrigerated for up to 2 days.
You could also serve this in taco shells, or in lettuce cups.

#  Beautiful Shredded Brisket

We shred this beautiful brisket and serve it in the lovely rich gravy with mashed potatoes or bread rolls. It's a favourite with the kids in our home!

**Preparation** 10 mins • **Cook** 8 hours • **Cooker capacity** 3.5 litres • **Serves** 6

1 large brown onion, diced
1 heaped teaspoon minced garlic
¼ cup tomato paste (concentrated puree)
1 tablespoon Dijon mustard
1.5 kg (3 lb 5 oz) piece beef brisket (not brined or corned)
¼ cup gravy powder (50 g)
1 teaspoon cracked black pepper

1. Place the onion and garlic over the base of the slow cooker bowl.

2. Combine the tomato paste and mustard and rub over the brisket.

3. Combine the gravy powder and pepper in a large plastic bag. Add the coated brisket to the bag and shake to coat the meat with powder mix.

4. Remove the brisket from the bag and sit it on top of the onion and garlic.

5. Cover and cook on low for 8 hours.

6. Transfer the meat to a chopping board. Use 2 forks to shred the meat. Return the meat to the slow cooker and stir to combine it with the cooking sauce.

# Mango Coconut Curried Sausages

This is a family-friendly, mild sausage curry packed with flavour and a touch of mango that everyone will love! For me, it's got three things going for it: it contains favourite fruit in the world, I love a good curry, and my kids love sausages so I know we'll have a hassle-free dinner time with everyone eating without complaints. Serve with brown rice or mash and vegetables.

**Preparation** 15 mins • **Cook** 6 hours • **Cooker capacity** 6 litres • **Serves** 6

12 thin sausages (beef or chicken), chopped into bite-sized pieces
1 brown onion, diced
425 g (15 oz) can mango pieces in syrup
400 ml (13½ fl oz) can coconut milk
1 tablespoon minced garlic
1 tablespoon curry powder
1 tablespoon cornflour (cornstarch)
1 cup sliced green onions/scallions/eschallots

1. Place the sausages and onion into the slow cooker.

2. Use a stick blender or food processor to blend the mango and syrup to a puree. Add the remaining ingredients (except the green onions) and blitz again until well combined.

3. Pour the mango mixture over the sausages.

4. Cover and cook on low for 5½ hours.

5. Add the green onions and cook for a further 30 minutes.

**Note:** This is a medium heat curry. You could halve the curry powder to reduce it to a mild heat. Alternatively, take out the children's serves and mix through ½ cup pouring cream to reduce the heat to mild, before plating them.

# Satay Pulled Pork Poutine

This recipe is inspired by the Canadian classic dish called poutine (hot chips topped with cheese and gravy) and our own Supercharged Satay Chicken recipe (see page 214). You can of course skip the chips and cheese and just serve this as satay pulled pork if you prefer.

**Preparation** 20 mins • **Cook** 7 hours • **Cooker capacity** 6 litres • **Serves** 8

1–1.5 kg (2 lb 3 oz–3 lb 5 oz) boneless pork roast
1 small brown onion, diced
1 tablespoon minced garlic
270 ml (9½ fl oz) can coconut cream
¾ cup smooth peanut butter
1 tablespoon sweet chilli sauce
¼ cup kecap manis (sweet soy sauce)
2 teaspoons soy sauce
1 tablespoon brown sugar
1 teaspoon fish sauce
Crispy French fries or potato wedges, to serve
Grated cheddar or mozzarella (1–2 cups depending on numbers of serves), to serve

1. Remove any netting or string from the pork, and place fat (rind) side down in the slow cooker.

2. Use a stick blender to combine the remaining ingredients, then pour over the pork.

3. Cover and cook on high for 6½ hours.

4. Lift the pork from the slow cooker. Remove and discard the fat layer, then shred the meat. Return the meat to the slow cooker. Cover and cook for a further 30 minutes on low.

5. Plate up the crispy fries or wedges, spoon over the pulled pork and top with cheese. If you like, pop the plates into a hot oven or give them a quick blast in the microwave to melt the cheese.

6. Serve hot and with a hearty appetite!

**Note:** If you want to extend the cooking time you could cook the pork on low, but you'll need a good 8–10 hours for a lovely tender result that will easily pull apart.

# Mexican Stuffed Capsicums

I had never eaten stuffed capsicums before this recipe – now I'm wondering why I waited so long! This is family-friendly but if you like a little heat you could always add some chilli powder to the stuffing. They are perfect on their own as a filling and flavour-packed meal with the sauce around them and the garnishes on top. They look AMAZING when plated, with all the vibrant colours, so this is a perfect meal to impress your next dinner guests!

**Preparation** 20 mins • **Cook** 5 hours • **Cooker capacity** 3.5 litres • **Serves** 3

3 large capsicums (peppers) (see note)
250 g (9 oz) minced (ground) lean pork
1 cup cooked basmati rice
1 large corn cob, kernels sliced off with a sharp knife
35 g (1¼ oz) sachet taco seasoning
400 g (14 oz) enchilada sauce
Sour cream, diced avocado and fresh coriander leaves, to serve

1. Carefully slice off just the top section of each capsicum to form the 'lid' of each one. Gently scoop out the seeds and membrane without damaging the capsicum shell.

2. Place the mince, cooked rice, corn kernels and taco seasoning into a large mixing bowl. Mix well to combine. Gently fill the capsicums with the mince mixture, and replace the 'lids'.

3. Pour the enchilada sauce into the slow cooker.

4. Gently sit the capsicums upright in the sauce. You may need to lean them against each other or against the sides but try to keep them all upright throughout cooking where possible.

5. Cover and cook on low for 5 hours.

6. Serve each capsicum in a shallow bowl, and spoon the sauce around the base to cover the bottom of the bowl.

7. Place a lid to the side of each capsicum so you can garnish the open top. Mixing up the colour of the capsicums and their lids looks amazing.

8. Top each capsicum with a dollop of sour cream, diced avocado and a scattering of fresh coriander leaves.

**Note:** I like to use one red, one green and one yellow capsicum. Look for ones with flat bases (as much as possible) so they sit steady when upright in the slow cooker.

# Complete Roast Beef Dinner

This delicious all-in-one pot roast dinner takes all the hassle out of a Sunday roast. Super tender beef and an array of vegetables will fill your plate – just add gravy, and dinner is done 😊.

**Preparation** 15 mins • **Cook** 8 hours • **Cooker capacity** 6 litres • **Serves** 6

2 kg (4 lb 6 oz) beef blade roast (I use two 1 kg [2 lb 3 oz] pieces)
Seasoning of your choice (see notes)
1 teaspoon olive oil
100 ml (3½ fl oz) red wine (such as Shiraz)
6 (or more) baby potatoes, skin on
1 large sweet potato, cut into 3 pieces
3 large carrots, halved
1 large brown onion, left whole (peeled)
1 medium wedge jap pumpkin, skin on, cut into 3 pieces
6–12 Brussels sprouts (1 or 2 per serve)
1 bunch asparagus, woody ends trimmed
Gravy, to serve (see note)

1. Sprinkle the beef generously with the seasoning.
2. Heat the oil in a searing slow cooker, or in a frying pan on the stovetop.
3. Sear the beef for 5–10 minutes, turning to brown each side.
4. Turn the slow cooker down from searing to low. If using a frying pan transfer the beef to the slow cooker.
5. Pour the wine over the beef, then arrange the potatoes, sweet potato and carrots around the beef.
6. Cover and cook on low for 2 hours.
7. Add the onion and pumpkin, placing them around the meat. Cover and cook for a further 5 hours.
8. Arrange the Brussels sprouts around the beef and lay the asparagus on top. Cover and cook for another 1 hour.
9. After the 8 hours cooking, check that the vegetables are tender. You'll notice the meat has released a lot of liquid.
10. Transfer the roast beef to a chopping board and allow to rest for a few minutes before carving.

11. Meanwhile, divide vegetables among serving plates, cutting into smaller pieces as required.

12. Carve the beef and serve with the vegetables, and gravy of your choice.

**Notes:** For seasoning, I like a combination of paprika, onion salt, garlic salt and pepper, which can be bought as a steak seasoning blend. You can use any seasoning you like.

Replace the wine with stock if you prefer, but note that the wine doesn't give a strong wine flavour in the meat or the vegetables.

I like to leave the skin on the pumpkin as it helps hold it intact but it could be removed at serving time.

Feel free to vary the vegetables used to suit your taste.

Browning the beef before slow cooking is optional and could be skipped.

To make gravy, you could thicken the cooking juices with instant gravy powder in a saucepan on the stovetop if you like.

# Notes

# Set 14 Shopping List

**MEATS**
400 g (14 oz) diced bacon
4 large skinless chicken breast fillets
1.5 g (3 lb 5 oz) beef brisket (not the corned/brined variety)
12 thin sausages (beef or chicken)
1–1.5 kg (2 lb 3 oz–3 lb 5 oz) boneless pork roast
250 g (9 oz) minced (ground) lean pork
2 kg (4 lb 6 oz) beef blade roast

**COLD PRODUCTS**
300 ml (10 fl oz) milk
300 ml (10 fl oz) cooking cream
4 cups grated tasty cheese
300 ml (10 fl oz) sour cream
French fries or potato wedges

**FRESH PRODUCE**
1.2 kg potatoes
6 baby potatoes
1 sweet potato
4 onions
2 stalks celery
½ red capsicum
½ green capsicum
3 large capsicum – one red, one green and one yellow
4 large carrots
1 bunch onions/scallions/eschalots
½ red onion
1 tomato
1 large corn cob
1 avocado
½ bunch fresh coriander
1 wedge jap pumpkin
6–12 brussels sprouts
1 bunch asparagus

**PANTRY**
2 litres liquid chicken stock
2 x 125 g (4½ oz) cans corn kernels
1 cup low fat mayonnaise
1 teaspoons wholegrain mustard
4 tablespoons minced garlic
¼ cup tomato paste (concentrated puree)
1 tablespoon Dijon mustard
1 tub roast meat gravy powder
1 x 425 g (15 fl oz) can mango pieces in syrup
1 x 400 ml (13½ fl oz) can coconut milk
270 g cans coconut cream
1 tablespoon mild curry powder
¾ cup smooth peanut butter
1 tablespoon sweet chilli sauce
¼ cup kecap manis (sweet soy sauce)
2 teaspoons soy sauce (I prefer salt reduced)
1 tablespoon brown sugar
1 teaspoon fish sauce
1 microwave quick cook cup basmati rice
1 x 35 g sachet taco seasoning
400 ml (13½ fl oz) enchilada sauce
Steak seasoning mix
1 teaspoon olive oil
100 ml (3½ fl oz) red wine, eg Shiraz
Cornflour
Cracked black pepper
Salt

# Extras

# Set 15

Broccoli and Cheese Soup

Rustic Baked Beans with BBQ and Bacon

Supercharged Satay

Sweet Chilli Chicken

Savoury Mince

Rogan Josh Beef

Char Sui Roast Pork

# Broccoli and Cheese Soup

A great recipe to get extra veggies into the family in a delicious way! The one potato in the soup will help it to thicken, but if you prefer a thicker soup you could halve the stock. Serve with crusty bread rolls.

**Preparation** 15 mins • **Cook** 5 hours 15 mins • **Cooker capacity** 6 litres • **Serves** 4

1 kg (2 lb 3 oz) broccoli, cut into florets (see note)
4 cups (1 L) vegetable stock
3 garlic cloves
1 brown onion, finely diced
1 large potato, finely diced
1 teaspoon cracked black pepper
½ teaspoon salt
150 ml (5½ fl oz) cooking cream
1 cup grated sharp cheese, plus extra to garnish (see note)

1. Combine the ingredients (except cream and cheese) in the slow cooker.

2. Cover and cook on low for 5 hours.

3. Add the cream, then, using a stick blender, puree the soup until smooth.

4. Stir the cheese through. Cover and cook for a further 15 minutes, to melt the cheese.

5. Serve with crusty bread rolls and a sprinkle of extra cheese to garnish.

**Note:** I use 2 x 500 g (1 lb 2 oz) bags of frozen broccoli but fresh is fine. Remove the thick stalk. A nice vintage cheddar works well in this recipe.

# Rustic Baked Beans with BBQ Sauce and Bacon

As a lifetime baked bean super-fan, I was kind of surprised I had never tried to cook my own before these. Now I wish I had started sooner! These are so versatile that I've included serving suggestions to enjoy them for breakfast, lunch or dinner – baked beans for every meal.

**Preparation** 15 mins • **Cook** 6 hours • **Cooker capacity** 5 litres • **Serves** 6–8

5 x 400 g (14 oz) cans cannellini beans, drained and rinsed
2 x 400 g (14 oz) cans diced tomatoes
300 g (10½ oz) diced bacon
1 brown onion, diced
1 red capsicum (pepper), diced
1 garlic clove, minced
1 tablespoon Worcestershire sauce
¾ cup BBQ sauce
½ cup brown sugar
¼ cup molasses
2 teaspoons smoked paprika

1. Place all the ingredients into the slow cooker. Mix gently to combine.
2. Cover and cook on low for 6 hours.

**Note:** If you do not have molasses, you could use golden syrup, but you will find most major supermarkets have molasses and it's ideal for this recipe.

We serve our baked beans with crusty bread and topped with a runny poached egg. Here are some other suggestions:

Breakfast – Serve with bacon and eggs.

Lunch – Serve as a side to hamburgers and fries.

Dinner – Serve with BBQ steak, steamed corn cobs and fresh crunchy slaw.

# Supercharged Satay Chicken

There's satay, and then there is supercharged satay. I adore a good satay and I wanted this recipe to have some serious peanut butter punch to it! Goal achieved! It is beautiful served with brown rice and stir-fried vegetables. Leftovers also make a lovely filling in a pie or toasted sandwich.

**Preparation** 20 mins • **Cook** 2 hours 40 mins • **Cooker capacity** 6 litres • **Serves** 6

1.25 kg (2 lb 12 oz) skinless chicken thigh fillets, sliced into strips
1 brown onion, diced
1 heaped teaspoon minced garlic
270 ml (9½ fl oz) can coconut cream
1 cup crunchy peanut butter
⅓ cup kecap manis (sweet soy sauce)
2 teaspoons cornflour (cornstarch)
1 small red chilli, deseeded and finely chopped
1 tablespoon brown sugar
2 teaspoons soy sauce
1 teaspoon fish sauce

1. Add chicken, onion and garlic to a searing slow cooker (or frying pan on the stovetop) and cook for 5–10 minutes. There is no need to brown the chicken, just seal it and soften the onion. If using a frying pan, transfer to the slow cooker after this step.

2. Combine all the other ingredients in a jug and blend with a stick mixer to thoroughly combine.

3. Pour over the chicken mixture in the slow cooker.

4. Cover, putting a tea towel (dish towel) under the lid, and cook on low for 2½ hours.

**Notes:** This produces a lovely thick strong satay sauce. You can reduce the peanut butter to ½ cup if you don't like a strong peanut taste but we love it exactly as it is in our family.

You can swap the crunchy peanut butter for smooth if you prefer and add ⅓ crushed peanuts before serving.

The one small chilli (without seeds) isn't spicy, and our younger children happily eat this with no concerns. If it worries you, reduce or remove the chilli entirely.

# Sweet Chilli Chicken

This is a family friendly Chinese 'fakeaway' to cook at home and save $$! Serve it with homemade fried rice and steamed veggies such as broccolini or Asian greens.

**Preparation** 20 mins • **Cook** 4 hours • **Cooker capacity** 3.5 litres • **Serves** 4

1 kg (2 lb 3 oz) skinless chicken thigh fillets, cut into strips
2 tablespoons cornflour (cornstarch)
½ green capsicum (pepper), diced
1 cup sweet chilli sauce (I use the sugar-free version)
2 tablespoons honey
1 tablespoon soy sauce
2 garlic cloves, minced
2 green onions/scallions/eschallots, thinly sliced, to garnish
Sesame seeds, to garnish

1. Combine the chicken and cornflour in a large plastic bag and shake to coat. Transfer the floured chicken to the slow cooker.

2. Add the capsicum on top of the chicken.

3. Combine the sweet chilli sauce, honey, soy sauce and garlic and pour over the chicken and capsicum.

4. Cover and cook on low for 4 hours.

5. Serve scattered with green onions and sesame seeds.

#  Savoury Mince

This is as easy as it gets! There are lots of yummy ways to serve this. Try it with creamy mash with cracked black pepper and a scattering of fresh chives. Use it as a ready-made filling for pies, pasties or toasted sandwiches. Top it with mashed potato or sweet potato and grated cheese for a cottage pie. Or simply serve it with seasonal vegetables and crusty bread rolls. It's super budget-friendly, so it's great on weeks when things are tight.

**Preparation** 10 mins • **Cook** 5 hours • **Cooker capacity** 5 litres • **Serves** 4

500 g (1 lb 2 oz) minced (ground) lean beef
2 cups diced mixed vegetables (fresh or frozen)
1 brown onion, diced
2 garlic cloves, minced
200 g (7 oz) can condensed tomato soup
2 tablespoons Worcestershire sauce
2 tablespoons BBQ sauce
2 tablespoons tomato sauce (ketchup)
1 tablespoon instant gravy mix (I usually use roast meat or brown onion flavour)
1 beef stock cube
½ cup water

1. Combine all the ingredients in the slow cooker and season with salt and pepper.

2. Cover and cook on low for 5 hours.

# Rogan Josh Beef

While this flavour-packed, aromatic Indian dish is traditionally made with lamb or goat, we love a beef version that's a little lighter on the waist and the hip pocket. If you prefer you can swap the beef for the other options. This is a mild version suitable for the whole family. Don't be put off by the long list of ingredients – it's totally worth it! This is great for a weekend dinner party, paired with a glass of merlot and great company.

Preparation 40 mins • Cook 6 hours • Cooker capacity 5 litres • Serves 4

4 teaspoons olive oil
1 kg (2 lb 3 oz) diced beef (see note)
1 teaspoon ground cardamom
½ teaspoon ground cinnamon
1 brown onion, sliced into thin strips
2 tablespoons paprika
1 tablespoon ground coriander
1 tablespoon ground cumin
1 teaspoon garam marsala
1 teaspoon ground fennel
1 teaspoon turmeric
1 tablespoon minced ginger
2 teaspoons minced garlic
1 red chilli, deseeded and finely chopped
1 cup beef stock
170 g can tomato paste (concentrated puree)
½ teaspoon salt
½ teaspoon cracked black pepper
½ cup natural yoghurt
Steamed rice and fresh coriander, to serve

1. Heat 1 teaspoon oil in a large heavy based frying pan over high heat. Sear a quarter of the beef until lightly browned. Transfer to the slow cooker. Repeat to cook the remaining beef in three more batches, in 1 teaspoon oil each time (the small batches stop it from stewing).

2. Reduce the heat to medium. Add the cardamom and cinnamon to the frying pan and cook for 30 seconds, until aromatic. Add the onion and cook for 2–3 minutes, stirring, to coat in the spices and to soften slightly.

3. Add paprika, coriander, cumin, garam masala, fennel and turmeric and stir for 1 minute to coat the onions and release the aromas. Add the ginger, garlic and chilli and stir to combine.

4. Transfer the onion and spice mixture to the slow cooker. Do not rinse the frying pan!

5. Pour the stock into the frying pan, stirring and scraping the base to deglaze it and capture any spices left behind.

6. Add the stock to the slow cooker, then stir in the tomato paste, salt and pepper.

7. Cover and cook on low for 6 hours.

8. Stir the yoghurt through just before serving.

9. Serve on rice, topped with fresh coriander

**Note:** I like to use a casserole-type beef like chuck steak or oyster blade. Just avoid anything very lean as it tends to be a little dry.

# ═── Char Siu Style Roast Pork ──●

Tired of the traditional roast pork and want to try something new? This is the recipe for you! It's so succulent and tender with beautiful flavour. We like this roast with mashed potato or sweet potato and steamed seasonal vegetables. This recipe includes overnight marinating so do this step the night before you start cooking.

**Preparation** 15 mins • **Cook** 8 hours (+ overnight marinating) **Cooker capacity** 6 litres
• **Serves** 4–6

1.5 kg (3 lb 5 oz) boneless pork roast
⅓ cup hoisin sauce
⅓ cup honey
⅓ cup salt-reduced soy sauce
2 tablespoons rice wine vinegar
2 tablespoons brown sugar
1 tablespoon minced garlic
½ teaspoon Chinese five spice
1½ teaspoons red food colouring

1. Leave the fat and skin on the pork, but remove any netting. Place the pork piece into a large ziploc bag or oven bag.

2. Combine all the other ingredients and pour into the bag with the pork. Seal tightly and place the bag into a large bowl to catch any leaks. Refrigerate overnight to marinate.

3. The next day, remove the pork from the bag and place it into the slow cooker, fat (rind) side facing up. Pour the marinade over the pork

4. Cover and cook on low for 6 hours.

5. Remove the rind and fat layer and discard. Turn the pork over and cook, covered, for a further 2 hours.

6. Serve sliced, with a little of the cooking juices spooned over.

**Note:** This could be served with a traditional side of rice and steamed Asian greens. We serve it with steamed seasonal vegetables and potato and sweet potato mash.

# Notes

# Set 15 Shopping List

**MEATS**

300 g (10½ oz) diced bacon

2.25 kg (4lb 15oz) skinless chicken thigh fillets

500 g (1 lb 2 oz) minced (ground) lean beef

1 kg (2 lb 3 oz) diced beef (eg casserole, chuck, oyster blade)

1.5 g (3 lb 5 oz) piece boneless pork roast

**COLD PRODUCTS**

2 x 500 g (1 lb 2 oz) bags frozen broccoli

2 cups diced mixed frozen vegetables (eg carrot, peas, corn)

150 ml (5 fl oz) cooking cream

1 cup grated sharp cheese + extra to garnish

½ cup natural yoghurt

**FRESH PRODUCE**

5 onions

1 large potato

1 red capsicum

½ green capsicum

2 small red chillies

2 green onions/scallions/eschalots

¼ bunch fresh coriander

1 garlic clove

**PANTRY**

1 litre (2 pints) liquid vegetable stock

1 cup (250 ml) liquid beef stock

5–6 tablespoons minced garlic

1 tablespoon minced ginger

5 x 400 g (14 oz) cans cannellini beans

3 tablespoons Worcestershire sauce

2 tablespoons tomato sauce

1 cup BBQ sauce

1 cup sweet chilli sauce

⅔ cup brown sugar

¼ cup of molasses

2 teaspoons smoked paprika

2 x 400 g (14 oz) can diced tomatoes

270 ml (9 fl oz) can full fat coconut cream

1 cup crunchy peanut butter

⅓ cup kecap manis (sweet soy sauce)

½ cup soy sauce

⅓ cup hoisin sauce

1 teaspoon fish sauce

½ cup honey

sesame seeds, to garnish

1 beef stock cube

200 g (7 oz) can tomato soup

1 sachet instant gravy mix

1 tablespoon olive oil

½ teaspoon cinnamon

1 teaspoon cardamon

2 tablespoons paprika

1 tablespoon ground coriander

1 tablespoon ground cumin

1 teaspoon garam marsala

1 teaspoon fennel

1 teaspoon turmeric

175 g (6 oz) tomato paste (concentrated puree)

2 tablespoons rice wine vinegar

½ teaspoon Chinese five space

1½ teaspoons red food colouring

Cornflour

Cracked black pepper

Salt

# Extras

_____

_____

_____

_____

_____

_____

_____

_____

_____

_____

_____

_____

_____

_____

_____

_____

_____

_____

_____

# Desserts

Chocolate Croissant Pudding

Bananas in Caramel Sauce

Chocolate Nut Clusters

Baked Apples

Carrot and Walnut Mug Muffins with Lemon Mascarpone
Frosting

Black Forrest Fudge

Sticky Date Pudding with Caramel Toffee Sauce

Ginger Self Saucing Pudding

Chocolate Crumb Cheesecake

Triple Choc Mug Muffins

# Chocolate Croissant Pudding

After Christmas we had an excess of croissants left to use up, so this was the perfect decadent reincarnation of those! Thankfully they are available in stores all year round though so you don't have to wait until Christmas.

**Preparation** 15 mins • **Cook** 1 hour 40 mins • **Cooker capacity** 1.5 litres • **Serves** 4

4 croissants
½ cup milk chocolate buttons or chips
4 eggs, whisked
⅔ cup caster sugar
200 ml (7 fl oz) cooking cream
100 ml (3½ fl oz) milk
1 teaspoon vanilla
½ teaspoon salt
Thick cream or ice cream, to serve

1. Spray the slow cooker bowl lightly with oil.

2. Tear the croissants into chunks and add half to the slow cooker. Scatter half the chocolate on top.

3. Add the other half of the croissant chunks then the remaining chocolate.

4. Whisk all the other ingredients in a jug, then pour over the croissants.

5. Cover, putting a tea towel (dish towel) under the lid. Cook on low for 1 hour 40 minutes or until the egg mixture is set around the croissants and not visible as liquid when you press a spoon down the side of the pudding to look deeper.

6. Serve immediately, so the chocolate is still melted and gooey, and top each bowl with a dollop of thick cream or ice cream.

**Note:** If you use a larger slow cooker the cooking time will be shorter.

# Bananas in Caramel Sauce

This recipe delivers beautiful caramelised bananas in a decadent caramel sauce. Serve them with creamy vanilla ice cream to perfectly balance the sweetness of the caramel. The relatively short cooking time makes it the perfect dessert to pop into the slow cooker just before you sit down to your main course, so it's ready when you are.

**Preparation** 15 mins • **Cook** 40 mins • **Cooker capacity** 7 litres • **Serves** 4

4 bananas, peeled and halved lengthways
50 g (1¾ oz) butter
½ cup brown sugar
1 tablespoon apple juice

1. Line the slow cooker with baking paper and add the bananas, cut side down.

2. Melt the butter in a heatproof bowl in the microwave. Add the brown sugar and apple juice and stir to combine well. Pour the mixture over the bananas.

3. Cover, putting a tea towel (dish towel) under the lid. Cook on high for about 40 minutes, or until the banana is soft and the syrup is thick. Serve immediately.

# Chocolate Nut Clusters

These little mounds of YUM are great for kids' parties, school bake sales, family gatherings or any sweet tooth craving.

**Preparation** 10 mins • **Cook** 1½ hours • **Cooker capacity** 3.5 litres • **Makes** 12–15

500 g (1 lb 2 oz) unsalted peanuts
3 x 180 g (6 oz) blocks milk cooking chocolate
2 tablespoons smooth peanut butter
300 g (10½ oz) white chocolate chips or buttons
1 cup mini marshmallows

1. Spray the slow cooker bowl lightly with oil and add the peanuts.

2. Add all the other ingredients (except the marshmallows) on top of the nuts.

3. Cover, putting a tea towel (dish towel) under the lid, and cook on low for 1 hour.

4. Stir the ingredients well. Cover and cook for a further 30 minutes. Line a tray with baking paper.

5. Add the marshmallows and give the mixture a really good stir.

6. Working quickly, before the marshmallows melt, scoop out about ¼ cup of mixture onto the prepared tray to form a cluster. Repeat to make 12–15 clusters.

7. Place the tray into the fridge until set. Transfer to an airtight container and store in the fridge.

#  Baked Apples

This classic dessert, just like Grandma used to make, is perfectly suited to slow cooking. You can change it up by adding some sultanas, finely chopped mixed dried fruits, or chopped walnuts to the filling. Serve with creamy vanilla ice cream or custard.

**Preparation** 15 mins • **Cook** 1 hour • **Cooker capacity** 5 litres • **Serves** 4

4 large Granny Smith apples
¼ cup brown sugar
1 teaspoon ground cinnamon
2 tablespoons unsalted butter

1. Core the apples and then peel a small strip around just the top of each one to stop them from splitting during cooking. Place the apples into the slow cooker.
2. Combine the brown sugar and cinnamon in a small bowl. Fill the apple centres with the sugar mixture, pushing it in with a teaspoon. Top each apple with 2 teaspoons of the butter.
3. Cover and cook on high for 1 hour.

**Note:** The cooking time will vary depending on the size of your slow cooker and the size of the apples. In a large cooker that cooks hotter, the apples may be ready in only 45 minutes. In a small cooker, they may need up to 1½ hours.

The first time you make them just note the time they take in your cooker, so you'll know exactly for next time.

# Carrot and Walnut Mug Muffins with Lemon Mascarpone Frosting

These are amazing single-serve desserts that (between you and me) you might even want two of, ha ha! I make four at a time in the one slow cooker, but I've listed the muffin ingredients per mug, so you can easily adjust the quantities to suit your family. The frosting is enough to do 4–6 muffins.

**Preparation** 25 mins • **Cook** 1 hour 10 mins • **Cooker capacity** 5 litres
• **Serves** One mug per person

**MUFFINS (FOR ONE MUG)**
20 g (¾ oz) butter, melted
3 tablespoons milk
½ teaspoon vanilla essence
½ teaspoon ground cinnamon
¼ cup self-raising flour
2 tablespoons brown sugar
2 tablespoons grated carrot
1 tablespoon finely chopped walnuts, plus whole walnuts to garnish

**FROSTING (FOR 4–6 MUGS)**
150 g (5¼ oz) mascarpone
½ cup icing sugar
2 teaspoons finely grated lemon zest, plus extra to garnish
¼ teaspoon vanilla essence

1. Pour 1 cup of hot tap water into the slow cooker and turn it on high while you prepare the muffins.
2. Spray the inside of each mug with oil, or grease with butter.
3. Place all the muffin ingredients (multiplied by how many mugs you want to make) into a mixing bowl and stir until combined.
4. Divide the muffin mixture evenly among the mugs. It should fill around ½ to ⅔ of each mug to allow room for rising during cooking.
5. Sit the mugs in the shallow hot water in the slow cooker.
6. Cover, putting a tea towel (dish towel) under the lid, and cook on high for 1 hour 10 minutes or until the muffins spring back when pressed lightly in the centre.
7. To make the frosting, beat the ingredients until soft peaks form.
8. Spread frosting onto muffins and top with extra lemon zest and a whole walnut. Serve either in the mugs or spooned out into dessert bowls.

**Note:** Cool the muffins before frosting if you want firmer frosting, or add while still warm if you want it to melt over the muffin.

# Black Forest Fudge

If you love the flavours of dark chocolate and cherry then this is for you! Black forest fudge is a hit of sweet yummy choc-cherry goodness that will leave you licking your fingers. You'll find the glace cherries in the dried fruit section at the supermarket. If you can find cherry essence it could replace the vanilla essence for an even stronger cherry flavour. We cook all our slow cooker fudge in a small 1.5 litre cooker. Be aware that a larger cooker with fudge in it will be relatively empty and therefore much hotter, so will cook much faster – keep an eye on it if you use a large cooker for fudge. Remember to always cook with lid OFF for fudge.

**Preparation** 15 mins • **Cook** 1½ hours • **Cooker capacity** 1.5 litres • **Makes** about 40 pieces

375 g (13 oz) dark cooking chocolate
2 x 180 g (6 oz) blocks milk cooking chocolate
1 tablespoon butter
1 tablespoon vanilla essence
395 g (14 oz) can sweetened condensed milk
200 g (7 oz) glace cherries, half of them halved, half of them quartered

1. Line a 20 x 20 cm (8 x 8 inch) baking pan with baking paper.

2. Break up the chocolate and add to the slow cooker.

3. Add the butter and vanilla, then pour over the condensed milk.

4. Cook, with the lid off, on low for 1½ hours. Stir with a metal spoon every 15 minutes or so. When the fudge is ready you will often see a light crust form on the top that wrinkles up when you push it with a spoon. If you see this it's ready (which may be sooner than the given time), otherwise stop cooking at 1½ hours maximum.

5. Pour the fudge into the prepared pan. Immediately stir through the quartered cherry pieces and mix well to disperse them throughout the chocolate.

6. Decorate the top with the halved cherries, pressing them slightly into the fudge before it sets.

7. Place into the fridge for at least 4 hours, or overnight, to set. Cut into squares to serve.

**Notes:** A wooden spoon or any spoon with water on it can cause chocolate to seize so ensure the metal spoon is dry.

The fudge will melt if not stored in the fridge. After cutting it into squares, keep it in a sealed container in the fridge for up to a few weeks, or in the freezer for up to a few months.

# Sticky Date Pudding with Caramel Toffee Sauce

For years I'd heard of people talking about sticky date pudding but I had never tried it. Once I did, I wondered what had taken me so long! SO yummy! This moist sticky pudding is delicious served with its own caramel toffee sauce that is both infused through the pudding and drizzled on top. Add a big scoop of creamy vanilla ice cream too. We serve leftovers the second night with custard.

**Preparation** 20 mins • **Cook** 1 hour 20 mins • **Cooker capacity** 5 litres • **Serves** 8

**PUDDING**
300 g (10½ oz) fresh dates, pitted and finely diced
1 teaspoon bicarbonate of soda
1¼ cups boiling water
100 g (3½ oz) butter, chopped
1 cup (firmly packed) brown sugar
½ teaspoon vanilla essence
2 eggs
2 cups self-raising flour

**CARAMEL TOFFEE SAUCE**
300 ml (10 fl oz) cooking cream
1 cup (firmly packed) brown sugar
80 g (3 oz) butter
½ teaspoon vanilla essence

1. Place the dates, bicarbonate of soda and boiling water in a bowl to soak for 15 minutes.

2. Line the slow cooker with baking paper, with the paper coming up the sides. Spray paper lightly with oil.

3. Beat the butter, sugar and vanilla until creamy. Add the eggs one at a time, beating well after each addition

4. Add the flour and soaked date mixture (with any remaining water included). Fold through to combine. Pour mixture into the prepared slow cooker.

5. Cover, putting a tea towel (dish towel) under the lid. Cook on high for 1 hour 10 minutes, or until a skewer inserted in the middle comes out clean.

6. Turn the slow cooker off but leave the pudding to sit in the warm cooker while you make the sauce.

7. To make the sauce, combine all the ingredients in a small saucepan. Stir over medium heat just until it comes to the boil. Reduce the heat so the sauce simmers, and stir constantly for 5–10 minutes, until thickened slightly. Remove from the heat.

8. Use the baking paper to lift the pudding out of the slow cooker and transfer it to a rimmed serving dish. Poke holes all over the pudding with a wooden skewer. Slowly pour half the sauce over the pudding, letting it soak through the holes.

9. Slice the pudding and divide it between serving bowls. Drizzle each piece with some of the remaining sauce. Add vanilla ice cream on the side and enjoy this amazing sweet treat!

**Note:** Cooking times will vary between slow cookers because the larger the cooker, the thinner the pudding, and the faster it will cook.

# Ginger Self-saucing Pudding

My friend and nursing colleague, Sarah, is from England and spoke to me of her love for the ginger self-saucing pudding her mum Anne made. I've seen so many self-saucing pudding varieties cooked in slow cookers, but I'd never even heard of a ginger one until then. I set about making it happen, not even sure if I'd enjoy it, but WOW! I need not have worried, it was amazing! The soft fluffy cake and generous hot sweet ginger sauce are perfect served with a dollop of double thick cream. I guarantee it will satisfy every last sweet tooth at your table. Decadent and delicious to the very last spoonful!

**Preparation** 20 mins • **Cook** 1 hours 45 mins • **Cooker capacity** 3.5 litres • **Serves** 4–6

**PUDDING**
1 cup plain (all-purpose) flour
2 teaspoons baking powder
1½ teaspoons ground ginger
¼ cup caster sugar
¼ cup brown sugar
1 tablespoon golden syrup
50 g (1¾ oz) butter, melted
½ cup milk

**SAUCE**
2 cups boiling water
½ cup caster sugar
½ cup brown sugar
1 tablespoon golden syrup
1½ teaspoons ground ginger

1. Spray the slow cooker with oil.
2. Combine all the pudding ingredients in a large bowl and stir to a smooth batter. Set aside.
3. In a jug, mix all the sauce ingredients, stirring to dissolve the sugar.
4. Pour the pudding batter into the slow cooker. Use a spoon to gently spread the batter to cover the base of the slow cooker bowl. (Making a few circular swirls as you go can result in some pretty patterns on your final pudding too!)
5. Gently pour the sauce over the batter. Don't worry about seeing so much liquid sitting on top; by the end it will be cake on top and beautiful sauce below.

6. Cover, putting a tea towel (dish towel) under the lid. Cook on high for 1 hour 45 minutes, or until the cake springs back when lightly touched in the centre. The sauce under the cake is very hot so be careful.

7. Cut the pudding into portions, then use a slotted spoon or serving spoon to scoop it into bowls. Spoon over generous lashing of the ginger sauce and finish with a dollop of double cream. Serve immediately.

# Chocolate Crumb Cheesecake

When I came up with this recipe, it was the first time I'd ever made my own cheesecake, and boy is that knowledge dangerous for my hips now that I know how easy they are to make! I already knew how delicious they were to eat though! This one is sure to be a hit at your next dinner party.

**Preparation** 30 mins • **Cook** 3 hours • **Cooker capacity** 6 litres • **Serves** 8

Soft butter, for greasing
200 g (7 oz) plain chocolate biscuits
100 g (3½ oz) unsalted butter, melted and cooled slightly
500 g (1 lb 2 oz) cream cheese, at room temperature, cubed
2 eggs
⅔ cup caster sugar
1 teaspoon vanilla essence
1 flaky chocolate bar (or 30 g/1 oz grated chocolate)

1. Grease a 20 cm (8 inch) round springform cake pan with butter.
2. Process the biscuits to fine crumbs in a food processor. Add the butter and process again to combine.
3. Add the biscuit mixture to the cake pan. Use the back of a spoon to press down to form a firm even base.
4. Clean the food processor bowl then add the cream cheese, eggs, sugar and vanilla. Process just until combined.
5. Pour the mixture over the biscuit base and smooth the surface. Sharply tap the pan a couple times on a bench to release any air bubbles
6. Place 3–4 scrunched up aluminium foil balls on the base of the slow cooker, close together, to sit the cake pan on (it's best not to go straight onto the bowl base).
7. Sit the cake pan firmly on the foil balls, making sure it's level.
8. Cover, putting a tea towel (dish towel) under the lid. Cook on high for 3 hours or until the cheesecake is set when touched gently in the centre.
9. Gently remove the pan from the slow cooker and put it in the fridge to chill before removing the sides. Slide the base onto a serving plate and top with crumbled flake or grated chocolate.

# Triple Choc Mug Muffins

I love the perfectly portioned serves of a mug cake! These have a gooey choc hazelnut base with a fluffy chocolate cake top that will have you digging down deep to get every last spoonful. Use a nice large coffee mug so it doesn't overflow – you don't want to lose a drop!

**Preparation** 20 mins • **Cook** 1 hour 10 minutes • **Cooker capacity** 6 litres • **Serves** 4

⅔ cup self-raising flour
⅓ cup cocoa powder
⅓ cup caster sugar
2 eggs
½ cup vegetable oil
½ cup milk
½ teaspoon vanilla essence
4 heaped tablespoons chocolate hazelnut spread
4 tablespoons white chocolate chips

1. Pour 1 cup of hot tap water into your slow cooker and turn it on high while you prepare the muffins.

2. Combine the ingredients (except the chocolate hazelnut spread and the white chocolate chips) in a bowl. Stir to a smooth batter.

3. Take 4 large mugs and add a heaped tablespoon of the chocolate hazelnut spread into the base of each.

4. Divide the cake batter evenly between the mugs, pouring gently on top of the spread. Scatter the white chocolate chips on top of the batter.

5. Sit the mugs in the shallow hot water in the slow cooker.

6. Cover, putting a tea towel (dish towel) under the lid. Cook on high for 60–70 minutes or until a cake springs back when lightly touched on top.

7. Serve with a spoon long enough to dig down to the gooey chocolate bottom. Enjoy!

# Notes

## MAKE YOUR OWN DRY FRENCH ONION SOUP MIX

½ cup onion flakes
1 teaspoon onion powder
1 teaspoon garlic powder
½ teaspoon celery salt
½ teaspoon pepper
1 teaspoon dried parsley
1 teaspoon salt

1. Combine all the ingredients and store in an airtight container for up to 6 months. 40 g (1½ oz) is equal to one purchased packet of French onion soup mix.

## MAKE YOUR OWN DRY RANCH DRESSING MIX

½ cup powdered milk
2 tablespoons dried parsley
3 teaspoons garlic powder
3 teaspoons onion powder
2 teaspoons dried dill
2 teaspoons dried onion flakes
1 teaspoon black pepper
1 teaspoon salt

1. Combine all the ingredients and store in airtight container for up to 6 month. 30 g (1 oz) is equal to one purchased packet of ranch mix.

# Thanks

Thank you to Roberta and Lachlan and the incredible team at ABC Books/ HarperCollins Publishing who make every book a possibility. And thanks forever to the delightful and incomparable Brigitta Doyle who started it all xx.

Thank you to Simon, Felicity, Nikki and Victoria who assist me with running our massive Facebook group. From little things, big things grow. ☺

Thank you to my friends and family who support me along the way!

To Julie, my lifelong friend, godmother to our children, and all-round inspirational woman!

To Leah and Karen who bring me sanity and serenity on the daily.

To Donna and Kris.

Special thanks also to Toni who is my calm through so many uncertain and stressful times and who never ever fails to look on the bright side of every coin!

To my sisters Vicki and Debbie and my Dad who have walked through this life with me from the very beginnings.

Loving thanks to my groom Simon, the man I've done life with for the past 30 years, and our three beautiful children. You are my everything xx. *No one* understands the hours involved in every book's journey like my family do. The sacrifices, the stresses, and the blessings! I achieve what I can only because I have you all standing beside me.

Last but never least, thank you to every single member of our Facebook group and our massive online community. You are the people who share my love of slow cooking and continue to inspire the creativity and fun in slow cooking with me and each other every day. No matter how large we grow, our community is, and always will be, nothing without each and every one of you being a part of it.

x Thank you x.

# Index

# Previous books in the
# SLOW COOKER CENTRAL
## series

Slow-cooking internet sensation Paulene Christie is a busy working mum with a passion for sharing new and exciting recipes for the slow cooker. She now has more than 650,000 members in her Facebook group, Slow Cooker Recipes 4 Families, and a hugely successful website, Slow Cooker Central. The Facebook page is so popular that Paulene has a team of four people (including her husband, Simon) to help her administer the thousands of recipes and comments that are posted each day. Paulene lives in Queensland with Simon, their three children and 30 slow cookers.

www.slowcookercentral.com
www.facebook.com/groups/SlowCookerRecipes4Families